EXPLORING

"As Patty Paul shares her adventures ~~~~~~~ ~~~~~~~ ~~~~ ~~~~~~~ she reveals the scope and the immense beauty of the human spirit. Her book is a reminder that if we are willing to knock on dimensional doorways, an endless journey of self-discovery awaits. And if we dare, we too can fall in love with our courage, commitment, and our continual pursuit of the sacred within ourselves. Thank you, Patty Paul, for sharing your journey of healing and for shining a reminding light into each of us to do the same."
— **Ann E. Bossingham**, metaphysical teacher, trance channel, and healer

"Patty Paul has written a compelling memoir, taking her readers along with her on her soul's journey of self-discovery. Illusions of separation are dissolved, healing takes place, and she emerges—conscious, authentic, and awake. It is a rare gift to be given the opportunity to view the world of the unseen and gain greater illumination that we do indeed create our own reality."
— **Athena Demetrios**, author of *Walking Between Worlds: A Spiritual Odyssey*

"I love the variety of lifetimes described in this book, along with the beautiful insights and gems of wisdom shared in these stories. It's unlike anything I've come across in my 'spiritual adventure' reading."
— **Kendra Langeteig, PhD**, author of *The New Asian Home* and essays and stories about mystical experience

"Wow, that was good reading! It is beautifully written by a wonderfully expressive writer."
— **B. L. Overton**, Licensed Practitioner (ret.), Church of Religious Science

❖ ❖ ❖ ❖

"This book is a great deal more than the fascinating stories of Patty Paul's other lifetimes.

The book's vast array of lifetimes gives us a broad view of our global and historical reality at the same time each lifetime's fascinating story presents a wise teaching that the author brings forward in a clear and understandable way.

Patty Paul shows us how each lifetime she explores relates to her current life and is a piece of the bigger picture of her soul's journey. As her colorful prose pulls us into her adventures, we are taken into her past life experiences and their respective worlds.

Diving into the 'vast sea of consciousness,' by self-guided meditations, the lifetimes surface. Each one brings its unique wisdom and becomes an integral part of the greater whole of the being that is Patty Paul. And we are the better for it."

— **Shawn Randall, MA**, internationally renowned lecturer, channel, and author of *Connecting with Your Higher Self*

Exploring
OTHER
LIFETIMES

Memoir of a Soul's Journey

Patty Paul

IMdex Publishing
ImagineDesireExpect

Published in the United States of America by:
IMdex Publishing
PO Box 1803
6771 Warner Ave.
Huntington Beach, CA 92647

Permissions granted:
Adaptation of *Astral Circus*, oil by Bob Venosa, as the background image on this book's cover, used by permission from Martina Hoffmann, guardian of her late husband's estate. Contact: art@martinahoffmann.com Robert Venosa's website: www.venosa.com

Reproduction of *Light Center*, oil by Agnes Pelton (1961), used by permission from Diana Argabrite, Director, Euphrat Museum of Art De Anza College, Cupertino, CA 95014. Contact: www.deanza.edu/euphrat/inthemuseum

Aerial photograph of the 2009 "double helix" crop circle in Tägermoos, Switzerland, courtesy of photographer Flickr/Kecko.

Cover design and interior formatting: Lance Buckley
Proofreading: Derrick Drury
Author's photograph: Kevin Roznowski

LCCN: 2020914005 (print)
ISBN: 978-0-9642726-0-6 (paperback)
ISBN: 978-0-9642726-1-3 (eBook)

10 9 8 7 6 5 4 3 2 1

Contents

Acknowledgements

I am deeply grateful to these wise friends who helped me discover and understand many of the lifetimes presented in this book—and to their dedicated channels who made them available: Elanor channeled by Steve; Torah channeled by Shawn Randall; Lazaris channeled by Jach Pursel; Baratta channeled by Dale Carley; Art channeled by Michael Crisp; Dr. Peebles channeled by Athena Demetrios; and Ophelia channeled by Liz Medearis.

A special thanks to my dear friend since the third grade, Barbara Overton, my first link to metaphysics when we were young and my manuscript reader and enthusiastic supporter now, when we are not so young.

Many thanks to Kendra Langeteig, PhD, for her encouragement.

I am grateful to Martina Hoffmann for granting me permission to use an adaptation of *Astral Circus*, by Bob Venosa, her late husband, as the background art on the cover of this book.

My thanks also to Diana Argabrite, Director of the Euphrat Museum of Art at De Anza College in Cupertino, CA, for permitting me to include an image of *Light Center*, an oil by Agnes Pelton (1961).

I am also grateful to Lance Buckley for designing this book's beautiful cover and formatting its interior, and many thanks to his assistant, Beth, for her patience.

A special thanks goes to Derrick Drury, English professor, and proofreader, who did the final proofing of my manuscript.

Finally, I am eternally grateful for my many unconditionally loving unseen friends, whose insightful guidance is given whenever I ask.

Introduction

Dear Reader,

Exploring Other Lifetimes: Memoir of a Soul's Journey, presents the unique stories of more than thirty of my other lifetimes and the living, breathing relationship each one has with the lifetime I am now living. The ties that bind them are the issues and emotions they have in common. The process by which I meet each lifetime, get to know and understand it, and then integrate it into the collective whole—our greater self—is demonstrated in each chapter.

As I make my way through this Patty Paul lifetime, now and then I encounter certain "difficult" people and painful situations that arouse powerful emotions within me. Sometimes my reliable process of acknowledging, expressing, and releasing those emotions doesn't clear them away. Instead, I spend sleepless nights embroiled in the situation, trapped in a whirlpool of thoughts and feelings churning round and round within me. When that happens, I know that another lifetime—sometimes more— with similar experiences and emotional issues is resonating energetically with my current situation, and it is time to meet and experience that lifetime in self-guided meditations.

Out of the chaos of my inner turmoil I find peace by truly *understanding* the other lifetime, calming the waters with compassion, then embracing that aspect of me as an integral part of the whole being we truly are.

Like a stone tossed into a vast sea of consciousness, the result is a rippling of peace that impacts all my lifetimes at once. As they unfold in the telling, the lifetime stories in this book—each so unexpected and unique— clearly show how it all works.

I appreciate this opportunity to share my lifetimes and my soul's journey with you.

—Patty Paul

Chapter 1

A New Adventure

I savored the peace and quiet of that summer morning in 1985 as I sipped my coffee and enjoyed the warm air floating into my living room through the open French doors. No annoying alarm clock had awakened me. No office beckoned. It was Sunday and I could do anything I wanted. I ended up changing my life that day.

I needed to do some housecleaning and as I moved from room to room in my condo, my thoughts drifted to my brief marriage that had recently ended. Our parting had been by amicable agreement. I felt a wave of relief and gratitude that our relationship had ended so quickly and painlessly, unlike several others. This had been marriage number three for me, with an engagement and a couple of other long-term relationships also in my past.

As I thought about it, the question I asked myself was: "How, at the age of fifty and a widow for twelve years—thinking I am so much wiser and more experienced now—did I make the same life-altering, seemingly bad choice to get married that I'd made as an insecure girl of eighteen?"

I wanted the answer to that question.

I sat myself down on my living room couch and began an honest, sometimes painful review of my life from the time I was a child to the Me sitting on that couch.

I had always been deeply interested in psychology and human behavior and had been studying those subjects for years. But the truth was that I was good at analyzing others but never made the effort to analyze myself. This time it was different.

Among other things, I acknowledged how independent and self-sufficient I had always been from about four years of age when I left my grandma's care to live with my mother and her new husband. But I also recognized that there was this other needy side of independent-me that always had to have a man in my life. As a child I wanted a daddy. In adolescence I *yearned* for a boyfriend. Even as a responsible, self-sufficient adult my life didn't seem complete without a man in it.

But why?

Hours passed and I kept digging deeper; over and over asking myself How and Why.

As the memories came to me, I felt alternately sad, chagrined, and angry with myself. Had I really been that clueless? That desperate? I reviewed not only the circumstances of what had happened and how I had felt, but also the person I was *being* at the time. For the first time ever, I admitted that my drinking was more than "social" and it sometimes led to behavior that was irresponsible and unbecoming. A wave of embarrassment and shame swept through me. "I don't want to be that person anymore."

After being removed from my grandma's care to live with my mother, I had virtually raised myself. I never felt loved or accepted by my mother. The truth is she neglected me. I remember her telling little me about "survival of the fittest." Her explanation may have been over my head, but the gist of her meaning was not: You better look out for yourself—because you're on your own kid.

Although I didn't have the words to explain it, I had a deep-seated feeling that since everyone knows that mothers automatically love and take care of their children, and mine did not, there must be something inherently wrong with *me*.

It also seemed as though everyone but me knew the secret of how to belong, how to fit in. I compensated for my inept social graces by trying to look perfect, be perfect and please other people—especially authority figures—hoping that would make me acceptable. Even loveable.

As a young adult, I often practiced in my head what I would say in a conversation. I found that drinking eased my anxiety in social situations—until eventually it began causing problems.

Now, as these insights came to me, I realized that maybe I just never learned how else to be. As I began to let in feelings of understanding, compassion, and forgiveness for myself, a weight began lifting from my heart.

But what about my pattern of having romantic relationships—one after another—interspersed with months of longing to be in one? And those three marriages and my other long-term romantic involvements? It had never dawned on me before how different those men were from each other; older, younger, with vastly different personalities, interests, educations, and occupations. How odd that seemed now. "Wait a minute. (A flash of insight.) The one common thread in that string of disparate relationships is ME!"

I realized in that moment that if my life was going to change, *I* would have to change.

Right then I made two choices. The first was to learn *how* to change myself. The second was to explore my spiritual side—something I had put on the back burner while I raised my two children. Organized religion and that vengeful Father-God had never felt right for me, but metaphysics always had.

Within two days, extraordinary things began to happen. It was as though a door had swung wide open and information and opportunities began flowing to me. Right away, I heard about Shirley MacLaine's book, *Out on a Limb,* published three years earlier, and I knew I had to read it.

What stood out for me in that book were Shirley's accounts of attending events where wise non-physical channeled beings spoke before an audience. One being she mentioned was Ramtha, channeled by J.Z. Knight. I had no idea that such things were taking place or how I could participate. I just *knew* that somehow, someway I had to hear a channeled-being sharing their wisdom.

Soon after reading *Out on a Limb,* this surprising thought popped into my head: "I want to visit my friend Barbara for the weekend." I had known Barbara since the third grade but had never visited her after she moved to Colorado years before. Flying there for only a weekend—it was too soon to ask for time off from my new job—normally would have seemed a waste of money to practical me. "You have to go," said my inner voice.

I called Barbara to see if I could come for a short visit. "Sure," she said. Two Fridays later I took off from LAX and landed in Denver.

Barbara picked me up at the airport and as we headed to her place, I mentioned my interest in the channeled beings I had read about in *Out on a Limb*. I knew she would understand because she also was into metaphysics. Barbara had read MacLaine's book too—and it turned out that she had two video tapes of recent workshops given by Ramtha. She said that each video was about three hours long and asked if I would like to watch them when we got to her house.

"Yes, I would." And that is exactly what I did, even before I unpacked.

As I watched those videos, I was fascinated by the channeling process and by what Ramtha had to say, especially: "You create your own reality." I *knew* in my gut that was true.

After my visit with Barbara, time seemed to fly by. I began reading all kinds of self-help and personal growth books that were popular at the time. In September I attended a weeklong Ramtha retreat in Estes Park, Colorado. I took vacation time off from work to be there and Barbara was my roommate. About four months later I attended a Ramtha weekend seminar at a hotel close to my home in Orange County.

In the interim, I had been watching more Ramtha videos, which I rented from a local New Age bookstore owned by a woman named Chip.

After attending the local Ramtha event, watching many videos, and listening to Ramtha's audio tapes on wide ranging subjects, I began questioning the value of their teachings. I heard many inconsistencies and contradictions that didn't jibe with "You create your own reality," which I knew was the bottom-line truth.

One last time I went to the bookstore to return a Ramtha video and to rent one that Chip was holding for me. When I arrived, she told me the Ramtha video was not available after all. "But I think you'll like *this* one." She handed me a video of a talk given by Lazaris, entitled *Awakening the Love*. I recalled that MacLaine had also mentioned Lazaris, a non-physical being channeled by Jach Pursel. Obviously, this was the video I was meant to take home with me.

As I watched Lazaris' video, the wisdom and truths they shared resonated within me at soul level—especially "You create your own reality, no ifs, ands or buts." Everything I heard rang true as wisdom that I wanted to understand and live by. I knew that Lazaris was the one who could help me grow and change. That was in early 1986. Lazaris' final event before a large audience, took place about thirty-five years later. Throughout those years I attended a multitude of Lazaris' evenings, weekend workshops, and four-day intensives. I also listened to hundreds of hours of recordings and videos, either made at those events or in addition to them.

Most importantly, I was digesting and integrating what I was learning—actually *living* it—and using the many processes and techniques that were suggested to improve my life. In that way, then and now, I have been continuously evolving. The result has been increasing success, happiness, and unexpected opportunities. Oh yes—and magic and miracles too!

Through the years, I have also sought insights and guidance from a select group of non-physical channeled beings whom I value as wise and trustworthy friends. All of them support the concept of: "I create my own reality." I have learned a myriad of things from those beings' workshops and private consultations. I also learned how to channel for my own benefit—a most valuable and intimate resource for me—in weekly classes I attended for eight years, which were conducted by a wise friend named Torah, channeled by Shawn Randall.

Since 1986, I have been discovering and exploring my other lifetimes, often with the help of some of my wise friends. When writing about one of those lifetimes, I refer to the relevant channeled being as "wise friend" and their name, without always mentioning who channels them. The names of their channels are listed in my Acknowledgements section.

In 2004 I knew it was time for me to set off on my own path of growth and change—making my way across a virgin field of infinite possibilities. On this latter leg of my journey, regular consultations with a wise being (with whom I feel a special rapport) named Elanor, channeled by fellow-metaphysician Steve, has been an especially valuable source of insights and guidance in dealing with my personal issues. Many of those issues have been directly connected to other lifetimes of mine that have the same challenges.

When I started writing this book, I had no idea what an organic and interactive experience it would be. I soon found out as I began reliving and relating the story of each lifetime and how it was connected to things I was dealing with in my current life. I usually did several meditations to understand each lifetime more fully. The insights I gained by doing that also led to a deeper understanding of myself, and an opportunity for inner change and personal growth.

Unexpectedly and wondrously, exploring my other lifetimes and writing about my experiences has become part of an amazing adventure—one that began with those two choices I made on that certain Sunday in 1985.

Chapter 2

Three Synchronicities and The Bigger Picture

I often find that when I step back to look at the bigger picture—the greater meaning of the reality before me—seemingly unrelated events turn out to be synchronicities working together to create something entirely different. Something grand and wondrous. That's how it was with three things that happened some years ago.

The first situation involved a smoky hotel room, the second was a freak accident I had on a California freeway, and together those disparate events led me to a powerful, life-changing third experience that was far beyond anything I could have imagined.

In the autumn of 2006, my friend Marilyn and I were attending a personal growth workshop in Northern California. The event began on a Thursday evening and would end on Sunday afternoon. As usual, Marilyn and I were sharing a hotel room, this time at the beautiful Sofitel Hotel in Redwood City.

On Saturday evening, during a twenty-minute break, Marilyn and I went up to our room on the sixth floor to relax and freshen up. The moment we stepped into the room we both smelled smoke—strong cigarette smoke. My automatic reaction was to figure out who was to blame.

"It must have been the maid, or some other employee with a key, and they smoked a cigarette in here!" said I with righteous indignation. I even called housekeeping and made a complaint.

When our break time was over, we rode the elevator down to the lowest level where a line was forming to re-enter our meeting room, a large ballroom with seating for the several hundred people in attendance. I stepped in line behind Rhodes, a man I had often talked with at these metaphysical workshops we'd been attending through the years. I told him about the awful smell of cigarette smoke in our room.

"Maybe it was an unseen friend trying to get your attention," said Rhodes.

When I let in what he said, his comment brought me back to my basic truth and what I had been learning in all these seminars: *I create my own reality*. All of it. Always. With no exceptions.

I quickly realized that instead of asking myself up in the room *how* and *why* I had created this reality—the smoky odor—I had resorted to my knee-jerk habit of blaming someone else. Before I left the hotel the next day, I left a note for the housekeeping manager apologizing for mistakenly blaming the staff. I also forgave myself.

Two days after I returned home, I had my monthly first-Tuesday consultation with my wise friend Elanor, channeled by my friend Steve. I have always valued Elanor's insights and suggestions about various personal issues and experiences that have come up for me during the past month: the how's and why's of what I am creating, what I need to change within myself to change my reality, and how those things are expressed and reflected in the bigger picture playing out on the world stage.

Through the years, I have found that Elanor's insights have helped me know and understand myself at deeper and deeper levels. And following Elanor's suggestions has always expedited my personal and spiritual growth—usually in ways I could not have imagined. The ongoing benefit from doing this work has been the positive and exponential changes that occur— first within me, and then as reflections and expressions in my physical reality.

The first thing I spoke to Elanor about that Tuesday was the mysterious smell of smoke in my hotel room. "How and why did I create that?" I asked. Elanor paused for a long moment, and then told me that it was a signal from one of my other lifetimes, a shaman living in about

10,000 BC—who used smoke in his rituals—who wanted to communicate with me.

I asked for more information, but Elanor said I could find that out for myself. I knew it would call for a meditative exploration into my unconscious, a valuable method I often use to discover more about myself and my world.

I was eager to meet that shaman.

This was my experience in the first meditation:

As I stood in my sacred space, a forest clearing with a central bonfire blazing into the night sky, I invited the shaman to come forward. I sensed a presence coming around from behind the bonfire. It was a male, bare-chested, with long shiny black hair and reddish-brown skin who stood before me. He wore a deerskin loincloth and held a long stick with a thick bundle of grey leaves bound together by slender green twigs, which he used for smudging during sacred tribal rituals.

In silent communication I learned he was revered by his tribe as their spiritual leader and healer. His name was Hamrati and he lived in a region of what would one day be known as North America. His reason for contacting me was to help me access more expanded levels of consciousness far beyond my current boundaries; and that is what his smudging rituals would facilitate.

I invited him to begin working with me right then. With Hamrati's guidance and smoke ritual, I experienced a lifting of my consciousness into unknown expanded levels of the unconscious realms.

I don't have adequate words to describe that powerful experience and most of what happened is beyond my recollection. But it changed me.

For many weeks I continued to do meditations with Hamrati. Each time, I could sense my consciousness expanding exponentially further and further during his smudging rituals on that ethereal plane.

Now and then I would smell a whiff of smoke in my house and would know it was Hamrati seeking my attention. It was always my choice about whether I would meet him in meditation at that moment. I usually did so.

What I didn't know at that time was—thanks to this work I was doing with Hamrati—a powerful revelation was in store for me.

One Tuesday afternoon in January 2007, several months after the smoky room incident, I was heading homeward on the southbound I-405 Freeway, while listening to my audio tape of the consultation I'd just had with Elanor at Steve's place near LAX.

I don't recall the issues I'd asked Elanor about that day, but I remember they were important, and I was eager to get home to begin following their suggestions. There was some soul-searching to be done and several meditations to experience. I knew I would need to carve out some time to really focus on this work.

The afternoon traffic was still light as I drove my trusty four-door Corolla in the lane to the right of the fast lane, traveling at my usual freeway speed of seventy miles per hour. The I-405 is a major freeway going south from Los Angeles County to San Diego and it passes through Orange County where I live. Like most major freeways, it has a concrete center divider—a sturdy wall three or four feet high—separating north-bound and southbound traffic.

Even though I was listening to our taped conversation playing in my car's audio cassette player, I was paying close attention to the road in front of me. Suddenly I saw something ahead that happened in a flash yet seemed to play out in slow motion.

A vehicle several car-lengths ahead of me in the fast lane on my left, ran over what looked like a tire iron. That metal bar flew into the center wall, bounced into the air and—with a loud THWAK—hit the driver's side of my car's hood just where it met the top of the left fender. And there it was trapped—like a baton in the hand of a majorette.

As I watched it happen, I was aware that I felt no fear at all. No sense of being in danger. I just calmly witnessed it, fascinated by what was unfolding in front of my eyes.

I thought, "Wow! Look at that. That thing could have smashed through the windshield and taken my head off. But I didn't create that reality."

There it was—this three-foot long metal bar stuck diagonally in the hood just a few feet in front of me. It didn't interfere with anything mechanical, so I slowed down and eased my way off the freeway to an exit ramp in Long Beach. At the end of the exit road, I pulled into a gas station conveniently located there and parked my car to look at the damage. The bar was wedged diagonally under a two-inch triangular corner of the hood where it met the top of the fender. Again, I thought, "Wow! Look at that."

A nice man happened to be standing nearby and he checked my car's undercarriage for any visible damage or leaks. It all looked okay. He also let me use his cell phone to call my insurance agent. My car was drivable, so I carefully traveled the twenty miles to my favorite mechanic's body shop just a few blocks from my house. My strange hood ornament held fast.

I was impressed by how calm and peaceful I remained throughout this whole experience. Nothing disturbed me, not even the damage to my little tan Corolla. Actually, I kept thinking, "Now I will definitely be able to stay home and focus on the metaphysical work I want to do because I won't have a car to drive for at least a week." That is exactly what I did.

The body shop took photos for my insurance company, showing the metal bar jammed into my car.

About ten days after the accident, I got my car back, repaired to perfection and paid for by the insurance company. Meanwhile, all the metaphysical work I wanted to do was finished, with satisfying results (although I don't recall what they were).

A few days later, I was headed to another personal growth event, a workshop given by Elanor and Art, a wise being channeled by Michael Crisp.

Since 2001, some of my metaphysical friends and I had been attending these small Art and Elanor workshops held once a month on Saturdays at Michael's condo in Playa del Rey. I always got a lot out of the helpful

information and guided meditations offered by these two wise beings.
During the second half of each workshop, we were given the opportunity
to ask Art and Elanor questions and to talk about any personal issues.

As usual, I had arrived at Michael's place well before the workshop
was to begin so I took that opportunity to share my amazing bar-stuck-
in-car story and photo with Steve and Michael.

During the afternoon sharing time, I asked Elanor and Art about my
car's encounter with the metal bar on the freeway. I figured that since
Steve and Michael had seen the photo, Elanor and Art would have access
to it through their channels' unconscious (and mine too, for that matter).

After a long pause, Art said to me, "Patty, you are *so* protected." I
immediately understood the truth of those words.

During some reckless years earlier in my life, I had created situations (always involving alcohol) which could have effectively derailed my
life—or ended it. Even back then, which was well before I delved into
metaphysics, I sensed that something was keeping me safe.

I asked Art what they meant about my being "so protected." They
suggested that I discover the meaning on my own. I knew that doing a
meditation or two after I got home would be the way to find out, perhaps with Hamrati's help.

As it turned out, in the first meditation not only did I learn the meaning of being *so protected*, with Hamrati's assistance my consciousness was
expanded far beyond anything I had ever experienced. It expanded to
my soul's level of consciousness and I sensed myself standing as one with
my soul. What followed forever changed my perception of my current
life and all my other lifetimes.

When that meditation was over—and while it was still fresh—I quickly
wrote down my powerful experience and the very real emotions I felt
while standing united with my soul.

These are the words that flowed as a stream of consciousness:

*I stand in unity with my soul as a Spiritual Being in a domain of
expanded consciousness. An array of lifetimes is spread before us as channels of flowing energies. There on the right, an aspect of me...I recognize it...
this lifetime...the One with my name...the life-stream that we, my soul and
I, have just chosen to experience. Chosen too, a divine purpose for this life.*

Now...standing at its portal...that One is ready to enter the energy flow. So filled with hope and determination are they. So ready to seek their divine purpose...longing to embrace it. That One understands that loneliness, sorrow, and pain from love lost...or never found...await them.

They know that abandonments and betrayals, fear and rage and despair will be part of their experience. They know too, that they will forget their purpose...will go astray...reach dead ends...and often lose their way. They resolve now to be responsible; to make choices and adjustments that can realign their focus.

So there stands that One...undaunted, ready, and willing. How courageous they are! How noble their spirit! How honorable! How worthy of love and appreciation are they!

Opening now Our heart-space, we...my soul and I...allow emotions to flow...loving...appreciating...this noble One so courageous and vulnerable. And that One now receiving the flowing love...flowing into and filling them...just as their life's-blood will course through arteries and veins saturating, nurturing the human body...they are nurtured now by Our flowing love and appreciation for this beautiful One. This Human Being.

During this sacred soul-level experience, I learned that for this lifetime—my Patty Paul lifetime—I chose to encounter and process significant challenges and blockages and unresolved emotional issues that were remainders from other lifetimes, many of which I visited in meditation.

In order to give me the time and space in this physical lifetime to make mistakes and learn from them; to work with other lifetimes and to do whatever else was needed to change and grow and become *more*, I would be "so protected"—by the support and guidance provided by my soul, by my other unseen friends, and by my unknown presence. That protection has allowed me to endure and evolve in this lifetime.

The next section presents the stories of my five key lifetimes, each of which has certain positive and negative elements which influence all of my lifetimes. These five are among the first lifetimes I learned of many years ago from my wise friend Lazaris; and are ones I have often visited in self-guided meditations, in order to know and understand their unique stories and how each one impacts my present life.

Five Key Lifetimes
Influencing
Every Lifetime

Chapter 3

Maya

c. 37,200 BC
Atlantis, 2nd Civilization

This is the lifetime of one named Maya, a girl born into a tribe of hunter-gatherers living on one of three large islands created by the cataclysmic events that destroyed the continent of Atlantis, thus ending its first civilization in approximately 42,000 BC.

Maya's lifetime has great significance as it is my *first directional lifetime*, the one in which my spiritual spark was ignited in the physical realm of planet Earth. That important factor seems so unlikely, so unexpected, in this unusual lifetime—which makes her life-story especially poignant and powerful.

This is Maya's story:

One moonless night a dark-skinned man crept out of the great tent where the other tribesmen slept and slipped into the blackness. He made his way quickly through the trees to the small hut where Oma lay sleeping. No one must know what he was about, for they would surely taunt him for this folly.

Even he, this aborigine, knew not why he was compelled to visit her that night, for Oma was an old woman of thirty winters— far too old for childbearing. No tribesmen had come to her hut in many seasons. He didn't know, nor could he ever understand, that his was a role agreed to as part of another's grand destiny.

Nine months after that midnight visit, the old woman gave birth to a tiny infant, a daughter she called Maya. The birth itself was a fluke of nature, an anomaly so strange, so unheard of, that it caused a commotion in the tribe, for only tribal women from ages thirteen to about twenty-seven bore children—as many children as possible. It had to be that way for the tribe to survive.

A mother would nurse her newborn and care for it until the next one came along about a year later. Then she would surrender her infant to be raised by the collective tribal mothers, females who were either too young or too old to bear their own children. That way no breeders ever had more than one child at a time to feed, to wean and then relinquish.

A child would never know its father. Men simply serviced the women so that as many children as possible could be produced. It had to be that way for the tribe to survive. There was no sense of forming relationships or pairing off.

Bearing as many children as possible was most important because life was extremely difficult under the harsh conditions of the region. Half the children died within their first six months. Another quarter of them died before they reached the age of seven or eight. Only one out of every seven children survived to adulthood. That was the cruel reality of tribal life. However, everything about Maya and *her* life would be different, beginning with the strange circumstance of her birth to the old woman.

Because Oma bore her so late in life, Maya was her very last child and she remained with her mother for five years instead of just the first year. For that reason, Oma and Maya were bonded as mother and child. They came to know each other well and felt love for one another. Maya's childhood with her mother was a simple and happy life. Their relationship was like no other in the tribe, and Oma kept Maya close.

Mother and child lived together in Oma's crude hut beyond the trees at a safe distance from the rest of the tribe. Maya never saw the others, but she knew of them because Oma often fetched meat from the tribe when her own hunting failed. When that trek was necessary, Oma would tie Maya to a tree with a rawhide thong before setting off for the tribal camp.

Maya didn't understand why she was bound so, and always feared that her mother would never return. But if she cried out Oma struck her, so she wept silently until her mother returned. Maya didn't know that her mother did this to protect her.

Finally, there came a day when everything changed. It was time for Maya to live with the tribal mothers.

Oma was very old now—thirty-five winters—and nearing the end of her life. It was too difficult for her to care for Maya. Also, Maya was now five years old, and after all, in six or seven years she would be old enough to bear her own children, for girls matured early in those primitive times.

Maya needed to be trained to live on her own. She must learn how to dress a kill, dry its hide, and preserve its meat, and do the other things that would help her and her offspring survive.

Being born to an old woman and remaining with her for so long—those unusual circumstances alone had made Maya different from the other children. When she finally was turned over to the tribal mothers to be reared, it became evident that there were other things about Maya that set her apart.

Though Maya's dark hair and dark skin were just like the others' in her tribe, she had an unusual, yet endearing pixyish quality about her. She was small for her age and her almond-shaped eyes had a mischievous twinkle in them when she did something naughty that seemed to imply, "Yes, I guess I did it. I guess I made this mess."

Maya remained a sweet and adorable child, but as she grew older, she wasn't as attractive as the other girls her age. When she became a young woman of ten, eleven, and twelve years of age, the differences became even more apparent. She behaved not at all like the other pubescent girls. Although physically mature, Maya still behaved like a little girl.

Because Maya had been born so late in her mother's life, then raised by her until she was five, Maya's unusual looks and odd behavior were not noticed until she was turned over to the tribal mothers.

The cause of her uniqueness was the condition now known as Down's syndrome. Its symptoms made Maya seem cute and pixyish when she was four, five and six. Her mental incapacity to reason was not a handicap in those early years. But now Maya was almost an adolescent and expected to bear children. Though she was becoming a woman physically, she seemed strangely different from the other girls her age. While they were off having babies, Maya was still playing with the little children.

With her oddities now so apparent, Maya was ostracized by the tribe. Because her early years were spent alone with her mother, no one had been aware of her peculiar looks and slow development. If they had been, they surely would have killed her in infancy. Because the tribe had been unaware of her peculiarities, Maya had survived.

Maya became the object of their ridicule and teasing, yet in her childlike innocence she did not understand why and just laughed along with the others. That cruel treatment, however, did take its toll. And things got even worse for her.

A massive drought came upon the land. Hunting was very poor. Food was so scarce that the tribal people were starving—and they needed a scapegoat. They needed someone to blame, and Maya—so unlike everyone else—was their target. "You bring the bad spirits to us. We have no rain and you are at fault. You are some sort of demonic child. You are too strange. Too different from the rest of us, and you always have been different. The gods are punishing us because of you. We must kill you and give you over to the gods. Then everything will be better for us."

The tribal leaders made plans to sacrifice Maya to appease the gods—and the tribe. Maya understood none of this. She simply smiled agreeably. But Oma, now a very old woman nearing forty and almost dead, feared for Maya's life and wanted to protect her dear child. She must take Maya far away—as far away as possible—in the dark of night. That night soon came. While the tribesmen slept, Oma roused Maya and led her by the hand into the moonless night.

They traveled for days and days, going far beyond the flat-lands, traversing the arid terrain until they reached the black mountains. "The forbidden land" so feared by the tribe.

Since the old woman was dying and of no more value to the tribe and Maya was useless, when their escape was discovered, the tribesman did not search for them. "The child will soon be taken by the gods and the curse will be lifted. The drought will end," said the tribal elders.

After reaching a safe distance, far from tribal hunting grounds, Oma sat Maya down and tried to caution her not to follow her. She knew she would die soon and wanted to return to the tribe for a proper burial. "You must stay here now. Do not let anyone get near you. Run and hide if someone comes. Do you understand?" Maya smiled and nodded.

Over and over, Oma tried to make Maya understand that she must stay behind. But each time she tried to leave, Maya came running after her. Maya simply could not comprehend what was happening.

Oma knew she would die soon and now she realized that she must remain with her child until the end. She could only hope that Maya would be able to survive on her own, somehow discovering how to fend for herself. Soon, death did come for Oma.

Maya sat by her mother's still body throughout the long night. She felt so lonely and didn't understand why her mother stayed asleep, even in the daylight. On the third morning, Maya awoke with a hungry belly. She left Oma's body and wandered off to find food.

That was how Maya's journey of discovery began. This is what happened: After wandering off on her own, Maya actually survived for another four years—a feat that would have been difficult for a normal person in that harsh environment. It was as though Maya was somehow strangely, miraculously guided and watched over on her solo journey.

In her wanderings, Maya saw such beauty and wonder and majesty within the natural world that even with her limited intellect she began to sense something grander, something greater—something *more* that exists "out there." Hers was an innate knowing of that spiritual truth.

Although unable to understand it intellectually, when Maya fell in love with the beauty and mystery of nature, that emotional connection touched our soul and our spiritual spark was ignited: "There is something greater here that I cannot see and I must discover what it is."

The spark that was ignited in Maya's lifetime, became a flame that impelled our spiritual quest in the physical world, and it lifted us from the animal realm of mere existence into the human realm of spiritual awareness.

Our life's course changed direction, seeking, always seeking to learn more of who we are as a spiritual being. Because that spiritual quest began with Maya, hers is our first *directional* lifetime.

I have worked with the Maya lifetime many times through the years, going to her time and space in meditation to get a clearer understanding of her relationship with her mother and also to understand why the primitive and superstitious tribesmen reacted as they did, blaming her for the drought, wanting to sacrifice her to the gods. I helped Maya understand that because of their limited beliefs, the others simply didn't know any better.

In one meditation, I sensed that Maya's life came to an end one freezing winter's day. Without proper shelter from the cold, she simply curled up in the snow and fell into a deep and final sleep.

Another revelation for me was discovering the sweet and loving nature—completely without guile, without criticism or judgment of others—that those with Down's syndrome possess.

In my final meditation, I blended my energy with Maya's, becoming one with her so that I could share her reality as she lived it. This was our experience:

It is morning and we sit by our mother's dead body, unable to shake her awake. It has been so for several days and nights. The food our mother gave us is gone, even the extra bits in the animal hide pouch, and we are so hungry. A small spring has provided water, but now it is hunger that compels us to stand and walk away. There is no worn path to follow. Instead, we seem guided by an innate connection with nature that surrounds us. We set off now...making our way across the terrain.

We notice a narrow stream flowing from the spring. How it splashes over rocks and sparkles in the light! Delighted, we follow along the banks of the ever-widening stream. But wait...now a beautiful blue and yellow butterfly catches our eye. We have never seen such colors! It flits here and there, high and low. Captivated by its beauty, we follow the direction of its random flight.

The enchanting butterfly lifts higher, higher into the air toward the branches of a tree. Oh, the tree! We see familiar fruit hanging from its branches and remember our hunger. We easily climb the sturdy tree and reach its fruit. What a gift. Our empty stomach is soon filled. Some of the fruit goes into the pouch, just as mother had shown us.

Now it is early afternoon. A light breeze stirs a pile of leaves. Off go the leaves spinning and spiraling over the ground past the cluster of fruit trees, across a wide field dappled with wildflowers and toward a small forest. We join in the dance, twirling and whirling with the wind and the leaves, laughing with joy at the freedom we feel. (I experience these rapturous feelings.)

The sun is low in the sky now, and shadows are long. It is time to rest for the night. We find ourselves in the comforting arms of the forest near a clump of dense shrubs. We crawl into a small space beneath them, our shelter for the night. A pile of dry leaves provides a soft bed and some warmth. As we drift off to sleep, we feel protected and safe. We feel nurtured and loved. (I am filled with these warm feelings.)

Throughout the passing days and months, we travel deeper into the forbidden land, never encountering another human being. In the quiet solitude of our journey, we sense our deep and mysterious connection to all that is.

Oh, the beauty and joy and wonder of it all!

An image that remains is of Maya and me, blended as one, on a moon-lit night:

The endless sky is ebony and filled with a zillion twinkling stars. Overhead, the moon is full. We extend an arm and marvel at how it reflects the moonlight. We look up at the sky, at the glowing moon and brilliant stars–and somehow in that moment we wonder: How? Why?

In that moment we have an inkling that there must be something more than what surrounds us. Something more than mere survival. Something more that exists in the vast unknown.

Thus was born my spiritual quest to discover the more as a human being living a multitude of lifetimes on this beautiful blue planet Earth, always seeking to know more about who I truly am.

The bigger picture of Maya's lifetime:

The story of my lifetime as Maya is very sad, very poignant, very tragic—yet very beautiful. Because of those dramatic aspects and the strong emotions they elicit, it is one of the most powerful of what are called *first directional* lifetimes. For that reason alone, it has been an important lifetime for me to get to know and understand. However, the primary reason for knowing this lifetime is that it is the one in which I sense that there is something greater and grander than mere existence. That awareness transformed us from a human animal, simply surviving, to a human being on a spiritual path of self-discovery.

There are other reasons to know and understand Maya's lifetime.

In this first directional lifetime I chose the pigments, the basic colors I was going to work with in *all* of my lifetimes, regardless of the picture I wanted to paint, the life story to be lived, and the lessons to be learned.

The positive influences from Maya's lifetime are present in my current life; and they can be augmented to have greater impact. When I acknowledge and own them, those positive energies expand exponentially.

The negative influences from the Maya lifetime also come up in my Patty Paul lifetime, and each time they cycle around is an opportunity to recognize, acknowledge, and then integrate them into the greater being we are.

These are the primary negative influences present in Maya's lifetime:

A sense of being different–being the outsider: The one who doesn't fit in. The one who is laughed at. The one who is put down. Variations of this *outsider* aspect, with its attendant self-disparaging thoughts and feelings, have certainly been present in my current lifetime. For many years, feeling socially inept was especially crippling and I often used alcohol to suppress my insecurities. Over time I have learned to recognize when the "outsider" part of me, with its crippling thoughts and feelings, gets activated. Using my metaphysical tools and techniques, I acknowledge their presence, discover the emotional wounding at the crux of their distress, and then integrate that aspect into the greater being I am. My *truer* self. That process sets me free.

The issue of trust–distrusting myself and other people: When the tribe turned against Maya, that experience embedded distrust of others deep in our unconscious. Although she didn't have the awareness or the words, this was the underlying impact: "They were nice to me at first, and then they turned against me. They blamed me for the drought and for their hunger and made me the scapegoat. They were going to kill me." Maya had no conscious perception of that reality, but at a deeper emotional level its impact was felt. In this lifetime, learning to first trust myself, then to trust selected others, has been one of my ongoing focuses. As I continually open to expanded levels of wisdom, I trust myself more fully—which draws trustworthy people into my reality.

The issue of the fear of not knowing. Being the one who doesn't know: Maya felt that isolating fear as confusion because she lacked the capacity to understand what was taking place and why she was so different from the others. *They* all knew how to behave, how to fit in, how to get along, and she did not. Out of that inner fear of being *the only one who doesn't know* were born feelings of alienation and not belonging. That same issue is present in one way or another in many of my lifetimes. In my current lifetime, the adults in my family—especially my mother— kept secrets from me when I was a child. They knew important things about me, such as who my biological father was, but they kept me in the dark. They took those secrets to their graves. As a child, I *was* the only one who didn't know. That feeling stayed with me until I learned, through metaphysics, higher truths about myself and how I create my own reality.

The issue of love equals tragedy: In Maya's lifetime scenario, her mother's love led to self-sacrifice and loss—with a tragic narrative that goes something like this: "Because she loved me, she led me away. Because she loved me, her own life came to an end. That is what love is. Love is that kind of sacrifice. Love leads to tragedy. Love means sacrificing oneself for the sake of others." Those beliefs are aspects of being a martyr, a negative influence programmed into our unconscious and an obstacle to spiritual growth. The impact of Maya's mother sacrificing herself out of love for her child, initiated feelings of guilt about being the reason for her sacrifice and feeling undeserving of such sacrifice. Those same feelings around love have been major issues in my life. Once in a great while I still feel a tinge of guilt as a form of self-punishment whenever I recall a past mistake. Forgiving myself for that self-inflicted punishment is the remedy.

This is the good news: When I recognize what is happening (sometimes later, rather than sooner), own my responsibility for creating the reality, then really feel the emotions that have arisen from the depths of me—the remorse, self-pity, anger, whatever is there—then release those feelings to my higher self, a positive energy-shift tangibly occurs within me and in my personal world. That is how I dispel the influence of those primary negative energies.

These are the primary positive influences present in Maya's lifetime:

A sense of having passion and compassion: Feeling compassion and having a passion for life, make the difference between mere existence as a human animal trying to survive from one day to the next, and living as a human being who seeks meaning and purpose in lifetime after lifetime. That tremendous shift from human animal to human being spontaneously occurs in our first directional lifetime. That was when Maya's passion and compassion were born, the passion she felt for her spiritual adventure, and her compassionate rapport with small children and with nature. Perhaps the specialness of being a Down's Syndrome child, who was gifted with naivety and lack of guile, allowed her to feel compassion at an age when "normal" children were selfish and self-centered. Her condition was less about Maya's diminished mental capacity, and more about her ability to understand things in a different way and her ability to be *present*— openly expressing her joy, happiness, sense of fun, and her curiosity in the moment.

The capacity for happiness and to inspire happiness and joy in others: Those are positive qualities that emanate from a sense of fun and aliveness and vitality that were present within Maya—and they are inherent qualities that I also have.

The influence of nature: Even with her limitations, Maya survived on her own for four years in a harsh environment—a feat that would have been difficult for a person with full mental capacity—because she trusted nature's bounty to provide what she needed to survive. Maya relied upon the natural elements—earth, water, fire, and air—for protection and survival as she traveled her solitary path into the wilderness. With her intimate connection, that oneness with nature, she touched our soul; for the abundance and beauty of nature are expressions and reflections of the soul. That nexus between nature and soul has an influence upon all my lifetimes, in one way or another.

Having the qualities of leadership. Being one's own leader: Although she certainly had no followers—after all she was "that strange child," the outcast—nevertheless Maya had the sense of adventure, the courage and confidence, the willingness to be wrong in search of what's right, that are qualities of leadership. Maya was courageous, willing to set off on her own. She had a sense of direction as she followed her inner compass. She had a lofty purpose to discover *the more* of all that is, and the drive to fulfill it. She was willing to follow her own heart, create her own path while always seeking the unknown. In that way Maya was her own leader. Those positive qualities of leadership—being my own leader, without the need or desire for followers—also motivate and inspire me in my current life.

The four key lifetimes that follow each contain variations of the same primary positive and negative influences.

Chapter 4

Loren

c. 10,840 BC
Atlantis, 3rd Civilization

This lifetime is the bittersweet, yet heroic tale of one known as Loren, a female child born into extreme poverty to a young mother addicted to drugs and living in the slums of the city of Atlantis. She was born in 10,840 BC, near the end of the third civilization.

To set the stage, this is what I learned about the Atlantis that exists in that dimension of time-space, from a being-friend I once channeled named Aktar, and from visits to Loren's lifetime in self-guided meditations:

What remains of the original continent of Atlantis now consists of many mountainous islands created by the destruction of the second civilization around 28,200 BC.

The city of Atlantis is situated on one of the two largest islands. Its government, centrally located there, occupies many large buildings. A crystal pyramid sits atop the main government building which houses the High Council, the governing body considered a "benevolent dictatorship created for the good of all" by the majority of Atlantis' citizens—who believe what they've been told: "A *higher power* bestows the divine right to govern upon the High Council."

The civic center's paved streets are inlaid with colorful stones that create beautiful mosaic patterns. Buildings there are constructed of adobe type materials and have thick walls in light colors to withstand the tropical heat. All buildings, including private residences, are powered by electricity from generator crystals of assorted sizes, as required by the building's needs.

The small outer islands that are inhabited have narrow flights of steps that wind their way to upper elevations. Cobblestone roads spiral up the hills, much like those now on the Isle of Capri. In the midst of each business district is a town square with shops rimming its border and a central fountain that provides water for the village.

The people of Atlantis wear a variety of comfortable, loose-fitting clothing in light colors, with sandals on their feet, or boots in cold weather. Women often wear simple kimono-type robes tied with a sash—not oriental in style but more Grecian—and made of silk or cotton. Tunics are also worn by many. Weather determines such clothing and the number of layers needed. Children wear smaller versions of the same type of clothing. Men have more formal styles for business—loose fitting jackets over long skirts.

Vehicles, including automobiles, are aerodynamically designed and made of metal. They have turbine engines powered by electro-magnetic energy produced by a crystal sphere of appropriate size, kept in a special compartment. There are also boats and hovercraft, large and small, and hot-air balloons for air travel.

All of Atlantis is powered by electro-magnetic energy that emanates from five gigantic generator crystals situated on outlier islands, in a pentagram formation. They surround a central island upon which is located the sixth and largest generator crystal—the Grand Crystal.

The five outlier generator crystals are balanced by sound waves and are aimed in different directions as needed to provide power to the smaller crystal receivers throughout Atlantis. The powerful Grand Crystal is maintained by technicians supervised by high priests and is highly guarded, for it is the energy source for the outlier generators—and for all of Atlantis.

That is the environment in which Loren's lifetime unfolds. This is her story:

As usual, Loren awakes early after a restless night of little sleep and it is taking a few minutes for her grogginess to dissipate. This is the morning of her fortieth birthday, though she will have far too much to deal with to even remember it.

Fully awake now, she realizes something is wrong. It wasn't the pre-dawn chattering of birds in the tree outside her window that had awakened her, as they do every morning. It was the dead silence. In an instant, her memory flashes back to another ominous silence she experienced long ago as a child.

At fourteen, Loren's mother had rebelled against her strict, middle-class family and had run away to Atlantis, the capitol city on the largest island of Atlantis. Eventually her heartbroken family had given up on her.

The naïve girl soon discovered that she was unprepared to survive on her own in the big city. Before long, she was living in an abandoned tenement with a boyfriend—selling drugs to eke out a meager living and to finance their own addictions. Then she got pregnant.

When Loren was born, her young parents truly loved her and doted on their darling child for the first couple of years— until feeding their insatiable drug habits became their highest priority. Then little Loren had to learn how to fend for herself.

One day when Loren was three years old, she was outdoors playing with two of her little neighbor-friends when they witnessed an amazing thing—a beautiful blue butterfly slowly emerging from its cocoon. Loren excitedly ran into her house to tell her mother.

Inside the house it was so very quiet. She knew her parents were at home so she called out to her mother, but there was no answer. She kept calling, "Mama. Mama," as she went from room to room. Still not a sound. The eerie silence frightened her. Loren sensed that something was wrong.

She walked into the kitchen and there on the floor was a horrible scene. Her heart sank as she gasped in pain and shock. Both of her parents were lying dead in a pool of blood. Clearly, they had been murdered—perhaps in a drug deal gone wrong. As young as she was, Loren knew about drugs and murders. They were common in this seedy neighborhood of boarded up buildings and littered streets. Life here was dangerous and one had to be tough to survive.

The sight before her was so ghastly, so overwhelming, little Loren couldn't grasp the enormity of what had happened—and yet she noticed a kind of peace on her parents' faces. Something she had never before seen. Perhaps *this* was the only peace they had ever known.

Loren ran from the house into the street, crying out for help. Someone called the authorities. A kind-hearted neighbor woman volunteered to take her in for the night. The next day she was claimed by a relative—someone she never even knew existed—and Loren's life was forever changed.

Her mother's family was notified of the death of their long-lost daughter and a maiden aunt, her mother's older sister Derra, came to Loren's rescue. The aunt was in good favor with the family and she took Loren to her house far from the city. Aunt Derra was to be her surrogate mother and would raise Loren as her own—and her only—child.

At first it seemed as though a good life had begun for Loren. She was given all the advantages that she'd never had before: a beautiful home in the country, good food, nice clothes and toys. Her aunt doted on her and showered her with gifts. But there was an underlying problem that only got bigger as time passed, until it finally fractured their relationship.

Derra had neither the knowledge nor the inclination to be a good mother, no motherly instinct to nurture as a caring parent. A loving bond was never established between Loren and her aunt.

Although Aunt Derra did the best she was capable of, her latent jealousy and competitiveness toward her younger sister was often expressed in remarks such as: "See...I am giving you all the things your mother never gave you. I'm giving you all these beautiful clothes and a good education and a nice bed to sleep in and three meals on the table. I'm giving you things you never had before. I am a better mother to you than she ever was."

Instinctively, Loren defended her dead mother: "No, you are wrong! My mother loved me better than you ever could. My mother was right. This house, these fancy clothes are meaningless things. My mother was better than you are."

Aunt Derra and Loren had tremendous battles. The older Loren got, the worse they became.

Every so often, the exasperated Derra would blurt out cruel things: "You're just like your mother! You're no good. You're rotten inside just like she was." Later she would try to apologize, saying that she really didn't mean what she had said. But the pain inflicted by the intensity of her angry words could not be undone. All Loren heard was: "You're just like your mother."

Her aunt's remarks soon became a self-fulfilling prophecy.

At age fourteen, Loren ran away from her aunt's house and began living in the slums of Atlantis, just as her young mother had done. And like her mother, Loren was soon lost in drug addiction—and lost in relationships with other addicts.

Soon she got pregnant and gave birth to a son. Loren struggled to survive and to care for her child as best she could, but she never felt that she was doing a good enough job as a mother.

Loren begged for food and did whatever was necessary to get by—and to get drugs. Eventually her infant son was taken from her by the authorities. She took even more drugs to numb the pain from losing her child—probably forever.

Loren was virtually duplicating the pattern of her mother's bleak life—and she had an ominous feeling that she too, was about to die. Her fear turned into paranoia, exacerbated by drugs. She imagined that someone was going to kill her, duplicating the last act from her mother's drama.

Eventually Loren just gave up and it seemed that soon she *would* die. Emaciated, dirty and hopeless, she took a knife to kill herself—but she just could not do it. Instead, she chopped off all her hair.

Young Loren's death was not to be, for she was rescued by a caring friend.

That friend was an older woman who had been checking on her from time to time through the years. She was the kind neighbor who had briefly sheltered little Loren after her parents' tragic deaths.

"You are not going to survive if you keep on this way and I'm afraid of losing you," said her friend. "I am going to take you to meet some people I know. Friends of mine who will look after you. They can give you a new life."

Loren's friend took her in hand and introduced her to her new caregivers, a small group of metaphysicians who welcomed Loren into their home and into their "family." They nurtured her with love and kindness. For the first time in her life Loren felt cared for and safe.

Over time, these kind people led Loren to an understanding of herself and the world through a metaphysical perspective. She now viewed her world, her life's purpose, and her own spirituality in a new and empowering way.

What they gave Loren filled the emptiness that she had tried to fill with drugs. She was loved and accepted just as she was. No longer needing drugs to ease the pain of being different—being the outcast who didn't belong—she got clean. Her life, now filled with hope and purpose, turned toward a future with new possibilities.

There was a sizeable group of courageous metaphysicians living in Atlantis who held their meetings in a large cavern located in the hills outside the city. They met in secret, for they were deemed traitors by the authorities because they openly criticized the government for the injustices it perpetrated against the poor, the addicted, and the mentally ill.

The authorities rounded up those "undesirables" from time to time and shipped them to isolated camps located on several

remote islands where they would be "taken care of"—never to
be heard from again. Water wells could easily be poisoned.

Loren not only thrived in her new loving and stable environment, she became filled with deep compassion for others,
especially those who were less fortunate.

Seeing the damage and injustice that was inflicted upon the
forgotten ones, people who were just like the homeless person she
once had been, Loren decided to take responsibility for saving
as many as she could. She became politically active and spoke
out against the punishing conditions that the disenfranchised
had to endure. It was a courageous thing to do in these times of
martial law when such outspokenness was considered treasonous.

Loren's primary mission was to provide aid to those she knew
so well: the many young people, most of them drug addicts, who
were living in the streets and back alleys of Atlantis.

Over time, and with the help of her friends, Loren set up a
number of half-way houses—safe havens for boys and girls who
were trying to make the transition from a dead-end life to one
that had meaning. The work that Loren was doing was beautiful and brilliant—until it abruptly came to an end.

Through several meditations, I observed Loren's experience in the final
days of Atlantis. This is what happened:

"The birds are silent. What is causing that?" Loren wonders as
she quickly gets dressed. Just then the whole building begins
shaking violently from side to side. It rises off its foundation,
then crashes down in a shattering of glass and splintered wood.
Miraculously her ceiling stays intact. With a loud CRASH, the
tree outside her broken window topples over, its roots stabbing
the air. The birds had sensed what was coming and had flown
away hours earlier.

Earthquakes were common in Atlantis, but nothing like this
one. Loren is terrified—more for the safety of her kids in the
shelters than for her own.

She doesn't know that the final destruction of Atlantis has
begun. Earthquakes, tidal waves, the breaking of natural gas

lines, the release of pollutants, fires—it all will take place in a chain reaction that will soon destroy everything. Within weeks Atlantis will disappear forever.

When the devastation begins, Loren's only concern is for the kids living in the various safe houses spread across town. She must make sure they get out safely. The only way Loren can make her way through the city now is on foot. She runs from shelter to shelter—dodging debris on the buckling sidewalks and streets—checking to see if the kids have gotten out in time or if they need help.

As structures crumble and fall, a friend spots Loren picking her way through the debris. He runs to her and urges her to escape with him in his boat. She chooses to remain. Loren must make sure that some young folks in a nearby shelter have gotten out safely. As she makes her way there, not knowing if they are waiting for her or if someone else has led them away, she is struck by falling debris from a collapsing building.

Loren never makes it to that safe house. She never learns whether the kids were able to escape or if they died in that shelter.

Severely injured, she is pinned under heavy beams and slabs of cement, unable to move. Lying there traumatized and bleeding, Loren is filled with anxiety and guilt about the ones she could not save. Another tremor brings more debris crashing down upon her and she dies instantly—forever trapped in that lonely tomb.

The bigger picture of Loren's lifetime:
This lifetime of mine is profoundly powerful in many ways. It has some of the primary influences—both negative and positive—that have impacted all my lifetimes.

These are the primary negative influences present in Loren's lifetime:
A *sense of being different*: Being the outsider who doesn't fit in was manifested in new ways in Loren's lifetime, including her rejection of authority figures, dropping out of mainstream society, and becoming a homeless person addicted to drugs.

Distrust also was present: The sudden deaths of her parents felt like abandonment to little Loren. And Aunt Derra, the person who was supposed to rescue her, only lambasted her with judgment and criticism, which adolescent Loren took as rejection. Being abandoned and rejected were Loren's reasons for distrusting others. Her distrust became fear, then paranoia, trying to survive on the dangerous streets of Atlantis.

The belief that *love equals sacrifice that leads to tragedy:* This negative influence was reinforced when Loren gave up her life trying to save others.

The influence of *mother's love produces guilt*: Guilt was produced in new ways. Even though Loren was severely injured and dying, she felt guilty because she could not "save them all." As a young mother, Loren felt she never took care of her child properly. Never did it good enough. (That guilt is something I also felt as my children's' too-young mother.)

In Loren's lifetime, some primary positive influences were manifested in different ways:

Having *compassion and passion*: As an adult, Loren's compassion for the less fortunate and her passion to help them, motivated her to be an activist on their behalf.

Having *leadership qualities*: Loren took a leadership role by assuming responsibility for the safety and welfare of the street children. She set up a system of safe houses for them. She also spoke out against the inhuman treatment of the undesirables. Those things took inner strength, confidence and courage—qualities of leadership. She was an inspiration to others, who loved and admired her.

Some aspects of my Loren lifetime have a direct connection to my current lifetime.

From a wise friend, I learned that many who played a part in Loren's lifetime returned to play a role in my current life.

The one who was Loren's surrogate parent, Aunt Derra, lacked the sensitivity and knowledge to be a nurturing, loving mother. In my current life, that being came back as my mother, trying to get it right this time but failing once again.

The one who was Loren's son is my son now.

I was surprised to learn that many of those street-children who Loren helped in her lifetime, have stopped by in mine just to acknowledge me and to say "thank you" by making an appearance—and then moving on. When I heard that, I knew right away who some of those visitors were.

My favorite paralegal job was at a wonderful law firm in Marina del Rey. It was unlike any firm I had ever worked for or even heard of. Casual dress and casual hours were encouraged. Friday was movie day for one of the litigation teams. The real estate attorney I worked for told me to just go home whenever my work was completed. (As a responsible nine-to-five employee, I had a hard time wrapping my head around that, so each day I found busy-work that kept me from leaving too early.)

Many of the lawyers, secretaries, and other paralegals had crystals displayed on their desks or bookshelves. Over lunch, we often talked about metaphysics—each from our own point of view. A few years after I left that firm, some of those friends even came to my Barnes and Noble book signings.

My most poignant memory of those special people at that law firm is from my last day there.

My co-workers were gathered around me to say goodbye and one of the secretaries—a quiet young woman whom I hadn't gotten to know well—kissed the back of my hand. It touched me so deeply then—and brings tears to my eyes now as I write about it.

After my Loren lifetime, I returned to have a cluster of lifetimes—in no particular sequence—taking place in Atlantis, again near its end-times, in order to relive scenarios similar to Loren's, but played out in many different ways. A few of those lifetimes are also in this book.

The purpose of these *particular* lifetimes, chosen by my soul (as they all are), was to show the bigger picture of how and why such destruction is brought about, and ways to create alternate realities.

Chapter 5

Markos

c. 410 BC

Ancient Greece

I was first told about this key lifetime in 1991, by a wise channeled-being friend who gave me important details about it that explained why its darkness casts a shadow over all of my lifetimes—especially my current one. I was encouraged to get to know and understand this important lifetime, one of the few I chose to live as a man, so that its negative influence could be ameliorated. Through the years I have attempted several meditations to do just that, but always something inside me blocked any deep connection. In one meditation I did learn that his name is Markos.

Writing this book brought me to that impasse once again, but now I was determined to get past whatever personal obstacles stood in the way, for I knew this key lifetime was meant to be Chapter 5. I have finally been able move forward, but by an oddly circuitous route, for it took a few synchronistic events to bring about my breakthrough.

Early one spring morning in 2019, I peered out my kitchen window to see if the weather would cooperate with my scheduled tennis class. I was dismayed to see a pile of large chunks of broken glass in the street right next to my small front yard. As I left for tennis, I told the property manager about the glass and he said he would clean it up. When I returned two hours later, the glass was still there, so with broom and dustpan in hand I went out to get rid of the broken glass myself.

First, I bent down to examine the pile for clues as to who the inconsiderate person was that left this mess. What caught my eye was a dark purple tumbled stone resting against a brick edger bordering my yard. "Is this thing real or made of resin?" I wondered.

I value and collect crystals and other minerals because I know that not only are they beautiful, each one has a unique consciousness that emanates from higher levels of the universal unconscious. The conscious energies connected to the mineral kingdom, are wise being-friends (some call them *devas*) with whom we can communicate. I thought this purple stone might be such a mineral, so I picked it up.

As I examined it, my first thought was, "It's probably synthetic because why would someone just leave it here?" But I was savvy enough to suspect that if this tumbled stone was not man-made, it must have a special meaning for me because of its odd arrival in my reality. I intended to find out for sure.

The next day I went to my bimonthly appointment with my wise friend Elanor, with whom I'd been having consultations for many years. As soon as Steve, who channels Elanor, answered the door, I asked him what kind of stone this was in my extended palm. (Steve also happens to own a wholesale crystal and mineral business.)

"It's a black amethyst," said Steve.

Amethyst is my birthstone, but I'd never heard of *black* amethyst.

Now in his living room, I made myself comfortable on the couch opposite Steve in his armchair. Soon he was in a deep trans-channeling mode, and before long I sensed Elanor's presence. I asked Eleanor about this black amethyst stone and the pile of broken glass it was near. After a pause, they told me the stone was a "gift from my unseen friends" as a reminder of my connection to the mineral kingdom. (I have done healing work using crystals in many lifetimes.) The pile of broken glass was necessary "to get my attention," added Elanor. Hearing this touched my heart, for it reminded me that I *do* matter to my unseen friends and that they are aware of me—something I knew *intellectually* but didn't always let in.

Following my unseen friends' obvious hint to work with my crystals again, when I got home I decided to find the appropriate piece in my collection that would facilitate my exploration of this lifetime known as Markos.

As I stood before the display of crystals and other minerals I'd arranged on four shelves of a white bookcase in my living room, my eyes were drawn to a rectangular amethyst geode— about eight inches by three inches in size—on one of the shelves. I examined it closely and was surprised to see that its amethyst-purple coloring had taken on a blackish hue—just like the tumbled black amethyst I had found. The color-change was another hint from my unseen friends that led me to the right crystal to work with as I continued writing my book.

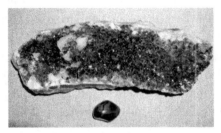

Black amethyst geode and tumbled stone

Now it was time to visit my heretofore elusive Markos lifetime.

Lying on my back atop my bed with the amethyst geode resting on my lower abdomen (second chakra related to creativity, passion, and sensuality) and the tumbled stone on the "notch" at the base of my throat (fifth chakra related to receiving and expressing communication), I did the first of many meditations to explore and understand the lifetime known as Markos. A lifetime so promising at the start but ending in a tragedy that haunts all my lifetimes.

Several meditations helped me to understand Markos, the man, and this story of his life and times:

Markos was born around 410 BC, during the Golden Age of Greece, to a family of great wealth and prestige in Athenian society. For generations Markos' family of prosperous sea-traders had been accumulating more and more land, making them extremely rich and powerful. Markos' father, the family patriarch, has great political clout in Athens. As his first-born son, Markos is meant to continue the family's legacy. It is his duty to do so.

As the eldest son of an aristocratic family, Markos would follow the traditional path for boys of such wealth and privilege. He was enrolled in a prestigious boarding school for a proper education. Eventually he was to become a philosopher of sorts, a fashionable endeavor in this age of the "philosopher kings"— as Plato once described them.

Upon completion of his schooling, Markos would enter the military where he was expected to follow the family tradition of having a distinguished military career, first as a great warrior leading his men into battle, killing many enemies, and then returning home as a hero. On some campaign he probably would receive some sort of wound—nothing major, just a sophisticated scar on his cheek or perhaps a slight limp—as a trophy of his valor. With a reputation worthy of his aristocratic station, his life would be one of affluence and leisure.

That was his father's plan, but Markos' life story plays out very differently. In a self-guided meditation, I witnessed what actually transpired:

Holding the reins of his weary horse, Markos carefully makes his way through the maze of mangled and bloody bodies slaughtered on this battlefield. Most of the dead were enemy citizen-soldiers—poorly trained foot soldiers with make-shift weapons, easily vanquished by his superior warriors. Markos looks at their faces contorted in agonized death. Many are so young. He is nauseated by the gore and heart-sick knowing the violence that had caused it. That he had caused. And this was only his second campaign.

Markos hates the killing and he hates the military. What do these endless battles in endless wars accomplish? Nothing! It is cruel and senseless idiocy.

"I can't do this anymore. It is too much. I am done with this!" he vows. It is a decision he has contemplated for months. He will resign from the military—then deal with his father's anger and disappointment when he returns home.

His choice made, instead of returning to his army's encampment, Markos gallops his horse to a pre-set rendezvous with his new friend, Conon, whom he met at a tavern some months before. During a long night of much wine and deep conversation they had bonded as kindred spirits who hated war and knew its futility.

Conon, a former cavalry officer, had also been revolted by all the misery and bloodshed of war. He understood what Markos was going through and supported his decision to leave the military. He encouraged Markos to follow his heart. "You are doing the right thing. It doesn't matter what your family thinks."

Conon had found an honorable way to leave the military, not as a deserter, but by resigning his commission through proper channels. Markos soon does the same.

Now as civilians, Markos and his friend are inseparable, like two musketeers traveling everywhere together, until the time comes for Markos to return home and face his family—with Conon at his side for moral support.

Markos' father is more than disappointed by his rebellion. He is enraged by it. He and the whole family blame his friend Conon, believing that he has somehow influenced Markos to defy them by abandoning, not just his military career, but also his duty to the family and its legacy.

"If we could just get them separated—make Conon disappear—then Markos will become the son we want him to be." The family plots to get rid of Markos' dear friend and ally, and some men are hired to carry out the deed.

In the dead of night, Conon is ambushed and carried off to a remote place where he is murdered. This is a time when human life has little value. If discreet, the rich and powerful can do whatever they deem necessary without censure or punishment.

After a few days, feigning ignorance, his father asks Markos where his friend is. "What happened to your friend? We haven't seen him for a while. Is everything alright between you two?"

"I have heard nothing from him." Markos is mystified and hurt by Conon's sudden absence.

After a month, more questions from his father: "Do you know anything yet? Have you heard from Conon?"

Markos remains silent.

His father persists: "Where did he go? He must have deserted you. What kind of friend is that?"

The family pretends to be concerned that Markos' friend has left him without a word. "Conon has callously abandoned you. Not even caring enough to say goodbye. You trusted him and now he is gone with no explanation. It's shameful!" says his mother.

Markos thinks it must be true. His heart is broken, and his trust shattered.

His father pleads with him: "Come home. We will take care of you. We are your family and you will always have a place here with us."

Markos moves back into the family household, grateful that they, unlike Conon, truly love him and care about his welfare.

It is only later that Markos learns what really happened to his friend. Servants' whispers overheard, a slip of a word here and there, a little investigative work, and finally Markos knows the truth. He is horrified to discover that his best friend has been murdered. By his own family! By his own father! Maybe not by him personally—but by his hired henchmen.

Along with shock and anger, Markos feels pangs of guilt. "I doubted my friend's loyalty. How could I have done that? And now he is dead because of his friendship with me."

Markos feels so betrayed by his father, so enraged at him, that in his fury he makes a silent vow to kill him. "He killed my friend and now he must pay with his own life."

That night Markos enters his father's bedroom fully intending to kill him.

They fight bitterly but the older man is no match for his son and he is soon thrown to the floor. Standing over his father, Markos raises high a heavy silver chalice to smash down in a crushing blow to his father's skull—but in a flash of clarity he realizes "If I kill him, will I not be as bad as he is? What right would I have to criticize what he's done if I do the same?"

Markos throws down the chalice, just missing his father's head. The clanging of metal on the stone floor echoes throughout the room as Markos turns and walks away.

As it happened, he had walked away forever, for Markos' life came to an end that very night. Overwhelmed by remorse and his family's betrayal, he simply sees no reason to live. He commits suicide by drinking poison. As he lies dying, his last thought is of punishing his father. "See. This is what you made me do."

This is the bigger picture of Markos' lifetime:
Markos' is not a pretty lifetime, with its negative influences outnumbering the positive. But it is an important one for me to understand.

These are the primary negative influences present:
Once more the familiar theme of *love leads to tragedy and loss* was played out in Markos' lifetime. Markos believed that the reason his friend Conon was murdered was because Markos loved him. That produced feelings of guilt.

Another primary influence, a sense of *being different,* of *not belonging,* is present in this lifetime. Markos rejected the life planned for him as a member of an elite family. That made him different. An outsider.

Being a martyr through *self-sacrifice as a punishment and as a manipulation to elicit guilt in others* is an extremely negative influence that is born in this lifetime. Markos killed himself to lay blame and guilt upon his father's head. His last thought was, "See what you made me do!" I now realize that this is the dark shadow over my current life that my wise friend was referring to.

The issue of trust: The *betrayal of trust* and the *distrust of men* are major issues in Marcos' lifetime. There was also confusion about whom he could trust: Conon? His father?

I learned a lot about myself from my Markos lifetime.
Seeing his trust issues regarding men, including the confusion about whom to trust, helped me realize that I had faced the same ones in my life. Now I could see that I had been harboring a *latent distrust* of men and, at a more pervasive level, a *distrust of all authority*—including

distrusting myself, the author of my own reality. Talk about inner conflict!

I realized, in retrospect, how my latent distrust had impacted all my relationships with men. Clearly this distrust issue was important for me to recognize, integrate and move beyond. And that is the process I repeated over time, until I felt I had moved beyond the need for it.

I learned something else that cleared up a mystery in my current life. The being who was Markos' close friend, Conon, reappeared in my present life as my stepfather Bill, whom I idolized from the time he entered my life when I was about two years old. In later years, he told me that I called him "Daddy" the first time I saw him. Bill was a huge influence in my life, but there was always something confusing about our relationship, for he was more like a mentor than a parent.

When I was ten years old my mother blurted out that Bill was not my real father—another complication in our relationship. Now I can see how the shock of learning *that* truth reinforced my distrust of men and authority figures, and certainly added to my confusion about who and what to believe.

Processing the issues present in my Markos lifetime has been incredibly important for improving my present life and advancing my journey. That benefit is the reason I explore my other lifetimes.

What follows are my last two key lifetimes, which are so different from the first three, for they are expressions of my more enlightened self.

Chapter 6

Mignon

C. 1100

Basque area of the Pyrenees Mountains

My fourth key lifetime is named Mignon, a female born about AD 1100 in Basque country, the French-Spanish region near the western Pyrenees Mountains. This is what I have learned from wise friends about her life and her destiny:

Mignon is born to a simple Basque farmer and his wife who have a small farm in the coastal farmland near the Bay of Biscay. Their life together is beautiful—idyllically peaceful and happy.

Mignon's mother is a homemaker—baking bread, cooking meals, weaving cloth—doing all the things that farmer's wives do. Her father toils on his fertile land to grow crops and raise livestock—chickens, pigs, cattle, and horses. He slaughters some of the animals to provide food for the family, others he sells in the marketplace. They are not wealthy, but they want for nothing.

Mignon is an only child and well loved by her parents. Hers is a carefree childhood devoted to playing and daydreaming. As she gets older her mother begins teaching her how to cook and make preserves, how to sew and weave, and do all the other things needed to be a farmer's wife, for that is a girl's destiny in this rural community.

Time passes quickly and soon Mignon is thirteen years of age, the time when girls are being considered as prospective wives by the local farm boys and their fathers.

In selecting a wife, the men judge a girl's physical qualities the same way they judge a horse. Does she have good teeth and a sound body? Does she have wide hips for easy birthing of many babies? Is she strong and sturdy enough for the hard physical labor on a farm? Those are the important qualities that a girl must have to be chosen for marriage. Being pretty or clever, like Mignon is, means nothing to them. She may be the right age to be a wife, but she does not meet the physical requirements. No, not at all, for Mignon is slender and very beautiful, with fine golden hair and soft skin. Her eyes are not brown as are most in this region. Hers are blue and have a sparkle in them. There is something aristocratic about her. Even her name means "delicate and dainty."

Mignon's unique physical qualities and demeanor are considered handicaps by the farm boys and their fathers. "She could never have children with those narrow hips. She'd be sick as a dog. And her hands are too soft for hard work."

The other girls of good peasant stock are already getting married and having babies, but Mignon is always passed over. Soon all her friends are married, and she is left behind. Secretly Mignon is relieved. She always knew she was different from the other girls and was glad of it. She never wanted to be some farmer's wife stuck in a predictable life. She *knew* she was destined for something else and trusted that her life would soon change.

More time goes by and Mignon, now almost sixteen, is rapidly becoming an old maid—a worrisome problem for her parents, for they are getting older and cannot afford to support her much longer. Luckily for them, an unexpected solution to their dilemma will soon appear right on their doorstep.

Seemingly from out of nowhere an old woman shows up in the village. She asks each person she encounters if they can help her. "I am looking for a slender girl with fair skin and blue eyes. Do you know her name and where I might find her?" The townsfolk don't take to strangers and are leery of answering this one's questions. They know this old woman is asking about Mignon. "But why?" they wonder. Would she cause harm?

A stranger in town is always news and there is much gossip. "Who is this old crone? What could she want with the girl?"

Finally, a tradesman offers to deliver the old woman to Mignon's farm on his donkey-cart, and before long they arrive at its front gate.

The crone's appearance will change all their lives.

The old woman rings the rusty bell hanging from a pole near the farmhouse door. Mignon's mother warily opens the heavy wooden door, for they seldom get visitors. She asks the stranger, "Yes? What is it you want?"

"I've been looking for the one who is your daughter. May I speak with her?"

The mother, cautiously curious, invites the old crone into the house and calls out to Mignon. "This woman is asking for you, daughter."

The instant she hears her mother's words, Mignon senses that this is the moment she always knew would come. "Ah there they are," she says to herself.

Not being used to strangers, at first Mignon is shy and a bit uneasy. For a time, the old woman and Mignon just sit quietly together at the kitchen table, delicately sipping their tea. The old woman resembles Mignon in many ways. She is slight of build, rather fragile looking, with soft skin and twinkling blue eyes just like Mignon's. After a while, Mignon feels so comfortable with this old woman that she no longer seems like a stranger and more like a long-lost friend. A friend she always knew would come for her.

The old woman speaks to the parents about taking Mignon on as her traveling companion. Someone to do her chores and care for her as the old woman grows older. The parents agree without hesitation. They love Mignon, but she is no good to them on the farm. She certainly is not fit for hard work, and they could not afford her if she became a spinster living off them.

The crone's offer to take Mignon off their hands is a godsend for all, and Mignon is eager to go with her. It is the adventure she has dreamt of.

The old woman leads Mignon away from the low-lying farm-lands, across terrain the girl has never seen before or even heard of, then up high into the foothills where the old one has a small log cabin. Outside her cabin is a large garden filled with the special herbs and vegetables she raises for herself and her patrons, who come from villages far and wide.

The old crone is well known to the simple folk residing in the area. They come to her for remedies and potions. When necessary, she will visit their homes to treat illnesses and wounds, usually in trade for a sack of grain or a plump chicken. In summertime she travels the countryside—now it will be with Mignon by her side—offering her services as a wise healer of body and spirit.

The old woman practices the ancient art of witchery. Besides being a successful healer, she performs great magic using crystals and other gifts from nature in her ministrations. The old crone is renowned as a powerful witch. A calling much respected in those times.

Her story is much like Mignon's. Once long ago, when *she* was a young girl, another wizened old crone had sought her out and had led her to the same hillside cabin to be her protégé. There she was taught the ways of witchcraft, just as she is now teaching those healing arts to Mignon—*her* chosen one. In time, the tradition will be carried forward by Mignon.

Under the crone's benevolent tutelage and care Mignon learns the sacred arts of witchcraft, including the ways of healing with herbal poultices and potions, and she becomes proficient in their many applications. The two of them do wonderful and beautiful things together—and great magic too—for many, many years.

Finally, the time has come for the old woman, now in her nineties and feeble, to pass on. As she lies on her deathbed, with Mignon bending close to hear her last words, the old one whispers that she will always be with her. And then she is gone.

Mignon doesn't understand the meaning of those words but she accepts the truth of them.

Now it is Mignon, a mature woman, who is the revered healer. The one whose services are sought after and appreciated by the country folk.

Mignon lives a long and purposeful life using the artistry of witchcraft. And one day, as an elderly crone, she too sets off on a journey traversing the land seeking, and being drawn to, that special maiden who will somehow be known to her and to whom she will pass along the ancient traditions.

This is the bigger picture of Mignon's lifetime:

Mignon's is a beautiful and powerful key lifetime. It is another moment in the continuum of spiritual growth that began with Maya's first directional lifetime—the one in which certain primary positive and negative influences were established which are present, to one degree or another, in *all* my lifetimes.

In Mignon's lifetime, it is the positive influences that are expressed.

Regarding the *issue of trust*: Mignon is gifted with a natural inclination to trust her intuition, and her destiny—even though she does not know what it will be. Because she has no need to know, or try to control what is going to happen, she experiences the wonder and beauty of trust and how it opens the way for new and unimagined possibilities. She is willing to let her destiny reveal itself.

As in my other key lifetimes, Mignon is *the outsider*. The one who is different. But this time it is accepted with grace. Her attitude is: "Yes, I am different and I relish my uniqueness!"

The *influence of nature* is very much present in Mignon's lifetime just as it is in Maya's. Mignon, following the traditions of witchery, uses herbs and crystals and other gifts from nature in her service to others. She is a healer, teacher, and inspiration to many in her lifetime.

Leadership–being her own leader: Mignon believes in herself and has the courage of her convictions to make her own way. A self-empowered leader who does not need followers.

The *capacity for love that's not tinged with guilt or martyrdom*: Mignon is well loved by her parents and then by her mentor, the old crone. With an open heart, Mignon receives their love and expresses her love into the world—in a sense, inhaling and exhaling love.

Now that I am an older and wiser "old crone," I feel a special rapport with my Mignon lifetime for we share the positive qualities of self-trust; of being unique with a sense of belonging; of having an alliance with nature through crystals and plants; and of being a self-empowered leader who doesn't need followers. And we have the capacity to love unconditionally.

I learned another thing about Mignon's lifetime that connects it to my own. The one who was the young girl she found as her protégé, returned as my daughter in my current life. This was comforting for me to know because my daughter has had a difficult and painful life.

I was reminded that a single lifetime is but a moment in one's eternal life.

Chapter 7

Morning Sun

C. 1450

Sioux Tribe; North American Great Plains

This important lifetime, my fifth and final key lifetime, is about a powerful Sioux medicine woman—a true visionary—known as Morning Sun. She and her tribe live on the Great Plains of North America, within sight of the majestic Rocky Mountains.

To understand this lifetime's relationship to the ones that I experienced before it, being open to the possibility that *all lifetimes are happening now* in the multidimensions of consciousness, will be helpful.

Think of a multiplex movie theater with different movies playing on a thousand screens all at once—and choosing which ones to experience, and in what order.

To help me understand this lifetime's significance and the choices that led to it, which were made by my soul and I (hereafter referred to as a united "we"), a wise channeled-being friend once described our journey in this physical realm. This is what I learned:

We entered this universe through the etheric portal of Sirius—as all consciousness does. Our first lifetimes were a cluster of them connected to the Sirius constellation. Next came a few lifetimes in the Pleiades. Then we focused on planet Earth, for we were aware of the harm being done on this beautiful blue planet by outside forces.

We saw how beings from Orion were callously inflicting great pain and suffering upon the animal and human realms. Mythological tales about satyrs (lustful creatures part man, part goat), fauns (part man, part goat), centaurs (part human, part horse), the Minotaur (part man, part bull), and the like, are faint echoes of the cruel experiments conducted by beings from Orion.

We chose to have lifetimes on planet Earth for the purpose of introducing compassion and other positive energies to offset the negative. The continent of Lemuria, a land that arose from the mists around 70,000 BC in what we know as the Pacific Ocean, was our destination, for it was created as a place for the Goddess's unconditional love, and harmonious masculine and feminine energies, to be expressed and reflected—making possible a new kind of reality for humankind.

We have many lifetimes in Lemuria in which we express compassion, understanding, forgiveness, and other healing human emotions. Those positive emotions are far more powerful than constricting emotions such as fear, anger, jealousy, hatred, and self-righteousness.

Finally, with the purpose of Lemuria now fulfilled, the land vanished into the mists around 60,000 BC.

Without physical evidence of its existence, Lemuria (which some call "Mu") is dismissed as simply a myth. Yet its energies echo still in the cultures of Micronesia, Melanesia, and Polynesia—which includes Hawaii and New Zealand.

Her grace remains, forever present in our physical realm and beyond. The Goddess—forgotten, but never lost.

Following Lemuria's disappearance into the ethers, we chose to remain on Earth as a mapmaker for humankind by starting over as a human animal in a primitive lifetime in Atlantis. That lifetime—my lifetime named Maya, in 37,200 BC—is the pivotal lifetime in which we transcend the human animal realm of survival-of-the-fittest, and enter the realm of human being with an awareness of our spiritual nature and a drive to understand what it is. Maya gained that awareness, making hers our first directional lifetime.

After Maya's lifetime, we make our way through a small galaxy of lifetimes in Atlantis dealing with different aspects of the same primal issues.

Then we return to Lemuria, having a few more lifetimes there. Next, we come forward to more recent times. Seeking, always seeking to discover more of who we truly are.

It is when we return to our native American spiritual traditions as the medicine woman Morning Sun, that we know: "We have found the way Home."

This is the story of Morning Sun's lifetime:

Around 1,450, a female child is born to a Sioux Indian squaw and her mate, a hunter, who are members of a tribe in the Dakota Plains. The loving parents named their papoose Bright Flower.

As the infant becomes a toddler, then a child of five or six, it becomes apparent that there is something special about her—a light in her eye, an uncommon wisdom—that sets her apart from other children.

The specialness of this child is soon recognized by the tribe's medicine woman. This gifted child is the one she has been waiting for; the child who will one day take her honored place in the tribe.

"To become an oracle and healer is her destiny." That was the word of the gods heard by the medicine woman.

When she is six years old, Bright Flower is claimed by the medicine woman to be her protégé. To be schooled in the healing arts. To be nurtured as a guiding light and prophet for the tribe.

The child's parents do not want to let her go, but who is to argue with this old woman—this powerful healer and visionary. And so the child will be raised by the venerable medicine woman, who renames her Morning Sun.

At first the little girl is afraid of the old woman, and homesick too. She begs to return to her mother and father. But as time passes, Morning Sun grows to trust and love the medicine woman, who now teaches her the ways and wisdoms of the Sioux Nation—with all its mysticism and heritage.

Through the years, Morning Sun learns about the stars, about Sirius as the portal to our universe—a belief very much part of the Sioux tradition. She learns about Lemuria, a mystical land where the gods once walked. These things and more are taught to her by the old medicine woman, who loves and mothers her as her own child.

The time finally comes when the medicine woman, now ancient and almost blind, will leave her physical body. After her death, the old one is honored by the tribe and burial rites are performed in the Sioux tradition.

The next day Morning Sun takes her place as the tribe's medicine woman in a sacred ritual performed by the tribal chief.

Many years go by and Morning Sun proves herself to be a powerful shaman and oracle, much respected by her tribe. One night she has a dream—a prophetic vision of things to come.

In her dream she sees a vast wave of white foam spreading across the land, pushing relentlessly up and over the great Rocky Mountains and flowing across the Plains until everything is covered. She knows well its meaning and she calls for a meeting with the tribal elders.

At the gathering, Morning Sun describes her vision and how it foretells the coming of the white man's tribe. How everything will change. How life for the Sioux will never be the same. She foresees the arrival of the first white men on the shores of North America, and their inevitable westward movement across the continent.

This is the bigger picture of Morning Sun's lifetime:

My lifetime as this powerful medicine woman is the last of my key lifetimes, for good reason. It is an expression of only the *primary positive influences*, without the negative. Morning Sun is an enlightened visionary with great healing powers for body and soul—a courageous leader and mapmaker showing the way Home. Morning Sun's is not a lifetime in which I set down my metaphysical powers, but rather one in which I pick them up again by returning to my American Indian tradition, which began with Hamrati's lifetime around 10,000 BC.

From several wise friends, I learned other things about Morning Sun's lifetime and its connection to my own.

The beings who are my son and daughter, also are Morning Sun's son and daughter. And the one who is the old medicine woman, returns again and again in many of my lifetimes as a mentor—sometimes in the form of an old woman, sometimes an old man—who offers wisdom and guidance.

I also learned that I could have chosen this fifth key lifetime to be my last one in the physical world, but instead I opted to return to participate in the grand evolution of consciousness and spirituality that is underway during *this* time and space on planet Earth.

I wanted to take part in the great adventure. I wanted to play!

Ties That Bind—
Lifetimes Related to
Present-Life Events

Chapter 8

Illusions and Enlightenment

A Visitor in June 2015;
and Ruda, Oracle in Ancient Greece

Ａs I begin this account of the events that unexpectedly opened the way to a powerful healing and greater wisdom for me, the date is June 3, 2015. This morning I was finishing my usual online activities in my home office when I heard an odd clatter of wheels on the asphalt street in front of my home. Curious, I walked through the hallway into the living room to see what had made such a noise.

Through the sliding glass doors and the white latticework enclosing my front patio, I saw a woman with long, straight blond hair standing in front of my place on the far side of the narrow street. Over her ample body she wore a multicolored tie-dyed tee shirt and an ankle-length skirt. Her left hand rested on the handle of a small, black, rolling travel bag standing upright behind her. Her left side was toward me, but her head was turned away.

Although I didn't see her face, I knew who she was—and I could hardly believe my eyes. It was my fifty-eight-year-old daughter, who had suffered a breakdown when she was a young adult and had been diagnosed as manic-depressive and paranoid-schizophrenic while in a psychiatric clinic. She refused to take medication after she was released and her condition just got worse through the years. I knew she had spent many years as a homeless person on the streets of various cities.

I was instantly filled with fear and questions. I started thinking of logical explanations for her presence and what might happen next. "How did she get here? Why is she standing there? Will she come to my door? Will she confront me with her usual raging tirade, blaming me for her terrible life?"

I dreaded having to turn her away again. I love my daughter dearly and feel such sorrow that her life has been so painful, but I had learned from experience that trying to help her or even communicate with her was futile.

Those were my thoughts and feelings as the human being I am. At the same time that inner dialogue was happening—as a spiritual being who knows that I create my own reality in this holographic physical world—I sense that her presence now is but an illusion. Different outcomes are possible, and I have the ability to manifest the reality I prefer.

I reacted in two ways.

As the human being so filled with apprehension, I took steps that seemed right in order for me to feel safe. Then I responded as an empowered spiritual being. I will describe those actions, and the rationale behind them—but first, some more pieces of this complex puzzle of reality creation:

It is obvious that synchronicity is in play. I am certain that seeing my daughter this morning is linked to what happened yesterday. That was when I had my bimonthly consultation with my wise and trusted being-friend Elanor, channeled by my friend Steve.

One of the issues I spoke to Elanor about was the fact that I was haunted by an image of my homeless and mentally ill daughter lying dead by the side of some deserted road. At a consultation in April, when I had asked about my daughter, Elanor had suggested that such a fate might soon be the ending to her life—which had spiraled deeper and deeper into the terrors of insanity despite all my earlier efforts to help her avoid it.

Elanor added that it was likely my small family and I would never hear from her again. Nor would we ever know what had become of her because she probably would have no identification when her body was found at the side of a road. I was heart-sick hearing those words, and my mind took a snapshot of that grim image.

After that April consultation, I processed the deep sorrow I felt for the loss of my beloved daughter—once so beautiful, intelligent, loving and compassionate—and the tragedy of her life as her once bright prospects had slowly been extinguished by insanity. However, this time, my reliable technique of feeling my honest emotions, then releasing them—sometimes in mediations, sometimes writing them down—didn't clear away the gray cloud of sorrow and dread that hovered over me. Nor did they erase that heartbreaking mental picture of her lifeless body lying by the side of a road.

I knew there must be something more for me to deal with. That's why yesterday I asked Elanor why I was still so haunted by that image, even after all my processing.

"How about some freedom?" suggested Elanor.

Elanor proposed that I find the lifetime of mine that is reflected by my daughter's, adding that I too have lifetimes where I am so lost in my mental illness that I meet a similar fate as a "Jane Doe." They suggested that one particular lifetime is very much like my daughter's. I also am lost in madness and through various circumstances I die anonymously by the side of the road.

That suggestion made sense to me. I was relieved to hear it and eager to follow it. I would visit that lifetime in meditation, as I had done with many, many other lifetimes, to get to know and understand that one (an aspect of multi-dimensional me) who is living it, and to reclaim and integrate them into the greater being we are.

The positive impact of this metaphysical work has always been immediate. It always releases the constricting energies of suppressed emotions—the ones I have been harboring and those resonating in the other lifetime—which sets me free to fully enjoy my otherwise happy and productive life.

I asked Elanor in what time and space that lifetime occurs.

"In early Greece."

"Do you have her name?"

"It's an unusual name. We're not clear what it is, but it has 'ru' in it."

When I came home from my consultation yesterday, I put visiting that lifetime on my To Do list.

Back to this morning: After I recognized the one standing in the street in front of my house as my daughter, I responded in two very different ways.

My knee-jerk reaction, born of fear—fear of being confronted by her insanity—was to lock the front and back doors, close the curtains and turn off the light. That was my Patty Paul, human being response, the one who had been subjected for decades to her daughter's rages and blaming, expressed in person or in lengthy phone tirades and emails—accusing me of conspiring with the government, the FBI, and miscellaneous others, to ruin her life.

Her anger intensified as she got older. When I learned that she had slashed her father's leather furniture with a knife, I knew I had to disconnect from her completely. That is what I did several years ago.

My second response to the sight of my daughter in the street was simultaneous with my "fear" response.

As my truer self, I was aware of both *the little picture*—the situation in my physical reality happening right now—and *the bigger picture*, a metaphysical understanding offering an opportunity to *consciously* create the reality I wanted.

With the wisdom of my truer self, I sensed intuitively that the vision of my daughter was an apparition. One clue that this image was not real: Although she knew where I lived and had been here many times in earlier years, the one in the street stood motionless, gazing at the vacant house across from mine.

Two relevant memories popped into my mind.

One afternoon years ago when I worked in Los Angles, I was driving in heavy traffic southbound on Figueroa Street through the seedy part of central L.A., where prostitutes stand on sidewalks hoping to catch the eye of potential customers on their way home from work.

The lane I was in was next to the curb where cars usually parked—but every afternoon that lane was opened to commuter traffic. I was going the speed limit of forty miles per hour, but very mindful of people on the busy sidewalk to my right.

All of a sudden, about twenty feet ahead of me, I "saw" one of the streetwalkers step off the curb right into my lane. I couldn't possibly stop in time to avoid hitting her. Rejecting that reality, I shouted NO! And— poof!—she vanished. In my rearview mirror I saw that woman still standing on the sidewalk in the same spot from which she had never moved.

I realized that the vision of her stepping off the curb was an opportunity for me, in that split-second moment, to choose my reality—a reality that had two possible outcomes—and to emphatically demand the one I wanted to create. Self-empowered in that way, I had imposed my will by saying NO! The result was spontaneous. (I do the same thing during an earthquake. I refuse to allow any of my precious crystals to get broken. It works every time.)

That was the first memory-flash that came to me this morning to remind me that I absolutely *do* manifest my own reality. The second was the case of the "vanishing lizard."

Early one morning a few years ago, I went out to my car parked in my carport to stow something inside the trunk. The first thing I saw was a large dead lizard lying at the entrance to my driveway, with its severed tail lying nearby and its bright red blood soaking into the asphalt. I was both saddened—I like lizards and I had recently seen this one, or its cousin, scurrying under some bushes—and repulsed. Cleaning up this yucky mess would have to wait until I at least had my morning coffee.

After two large mugs of coffee, which I drank as I read some head-lines, paid a few bills, and did a crossword puzzle online, I decided I had better clean up the dead lizard mess now—before it got worse baking in the sun on hot asphalt.

I threw on some clothes and went to the gory scene in the driveway. What I found was—*nothing*. No lizard. No tail. And no trace of blood anywhere.

I was more amused than amazed because I owned that I had mani-fested that reality by simply *allowing* my preference to be realized. I did NOT want to clean up the gory mess in my driveway!

Remembering those two earlier magical experiences reminded me to let go of the erroneous belief that everything must be explainable by linear logic. I know from experience that letting go of the need for stories and explanations opens the door to magical creation. And magic is always afoot.

I realize that the vision of my daughter this morning is a clear message that it is important for me to visit my Grecian lifetime right away. And that is what I did—more than once.

This was my experience in my first meditation:

Standing in my familiar safe place, I sense the presence of my soul and I express my desire to visit the lifetime of the one living in early Greece—the mad woman; my lifetime being reflected by my daughter's. I sense myself being transported through time and space until I begin to descend. I feel my feet on solid ground and I open my mental eyes.

It is midday and the blazing sun high in the sky bathes everything in bright light. I am standing on a cobblestone street in the agora, the public square surrounded by terra cotta structures that seem to be shops.

In the center of the marketplace is a cistern-type well—a source of water for the community—surrounded by a low terra cotta wall. Sitting upon that wall is a dark-haired woman shrouded in black clothing. It covers all but her wrinkled face and gnarled hands. She wears sandals on her dirt-encrusted feet.

She is talking to herself, sometimes mumbling, sometimes aloud, as she rocks back and forth. She spies me and glares through her crazed eyes. "Stay away!" she hisses.

"I came here to meet you and to spend time with you as a friend," I say. Opening my heart-space I flow love and compassion to her heart. I move closer and sense her fear subsiding. I ask her name.

"Ruda" is what I hear.

I take a seat near her on the wall and ask her to tell me about her life. As she speaks, I begin to witness her journey.

I learn that once she had been regarded by the priests as a savant who spoke in the many voices of the goddesses they worshipped; the voices of Athena, Artemis, Circe, Demeter, and several others.

She had held a respected station in her village then, and she enjoyed all the attention and adulation. In her madness, she believed that she truly was the embodiment of the various goddesses.

At some point, however, the priests turned against her, proclaiming that she had tricked them with her witchery. They denounced her and her gibberish. "You are filled with evil forces," they said.

(There was no knowledge of insanity in that culture, nor any treatment for it.)

In another meditation, I blend my energies with hers to sense what it feels like to be her:

I am filled with confusion and fear—loud voices all talking at once in my head. The noise is overwhelming. Reality is distorted and terrifying.

Returning to Ruda's lifetime—first as observer, then as participant—this was my experience:

After the priests denounce her, she is shunned by the villagers and eventually she is driven out of the village beyond the walls that surround it and into the desert wilderness.

She makes her way to a road—more like a dirt trail seldom used. For days she wanders along that dusty road. Heat from the blazing sun is oppressive and soon the water bag slung over her shoulder is empty.

Finally, she can travel no further. She collapses—soon to die by the side of this desolate desert road.

I go to her as she lies dying and cradle her in my arms. I consciously help lift her light-body out of her physical body—freeing the being she is from that dying carcass, a physical body no longer needed.

I guide this one into the white light of unconditional love and higher wisdom, to reunite with our soul as an integral part of the whole.

Before the conclusion of this last mediation my consciousness spontaneously expands to levels far beyond my Ruda lifetime:

*I sense myself being transported to a beautiful garden-setting manifested
in the ethers of the unconscious. There I reunite with the spiritual being
who had been my daughter.*

*Recognition, understanding, and unconditional love we have for
each other flows between us–bringing a wonderful multi-level healing.*

As my consciousness expands even more, I spontaneously open
to and receive awareness and insights from higher levels of
knowledge—dimensions accessing greater wisdom—with these
thoughts floating like snowflakes into my consciousness:

*Every lifetime is a dream–my soul's dream–and is no more real than
my nighttime dreams and nightmares.*

*Each lifetime is merely a story–like a fairytale or a movie–created
as an opportunity from which to learn more about myself–taking place
within the context of time and space in the physical world.*

*My night dreams and nightmares play out in a level of consciousness
where time and space may be telescoped, overlapping, and distorted–but
the emotions they elicit are the same emotions I have when I'm awake,
and have in all of my lifetimes.*

*The raw emotions, not the story, are the energies that form the essence
of a lifetime and a dream. Emotions are the only things that are real
and they precede everything.*

*The story is fiction. A story about who, what, when, where and why is
what I invent to create a logical explanation for having the emotions I feel.*

*The story is fashioned from my beliefs and attitudes and other raw
materials, as seen through the lenses of my imagination, desire and
expectation.*

*In my present Patty Paul life, when I create a story to explain by
linear logic what happened–or is happening–I am creating a structure
around that event to contain, confine, and control it.*

*When I assign blame (or otherwise give my authority and power to
another) then justify it–"They made me angry-sad-afraid." or "They
must tell me what to do-must take care of me-must save me."–and then
infuse my story with the energies of my feelings, I give that story substance.*

By telling myself a story–the reason or explanation–and infusing it with emotional substance, I make that story spontaneously manifest in my physical reality as form. When I focus my attention on the story– bring all the atoms together–I make it matter. I make the story become realized in physical form.

For decades I have been hearing similar truths spoken by certain wise and loving non-physical beings at workshops I've attended, and in private consultations I've had—but receiving them into my unconscious in that powerful meditation really brought them home for me in a new way.

Being gifted with these higher truths, and gaining a deeper understanding of them, was for me a priceless treasure of greater enlightenment.

—and it all began with a vision of my daughter standing in front of my house.

Chapter 9

Agnes and I

July 2009 in California; Sirius and Lemuria

O ne beautiful Southern California morning in mid-July 2009, I was online scanning front page articles in our local newspaper, the Orange County Register. An item about a current exhibit at the Orange County Museum of Art in nearby Newport Beach caught my attention. The title of the exhibit was "Illumination." That word rang my metaphysical chimes!

As I read the article, I was further intrigued to learn that the exhibit featured paintings by four women, the most famous of them being Georgia O'Keeffe. Although the four artists had different styles, each was inspired by nature and all used "Illumination to convey transcendence and spirituality."

Besides O'Keeffe (1887–1986), the other American artists featured in this show were Agnes Pelton (1881–1961), Agnes Martin (1912–2004), and Florence Miller Pierce (1918–2007). I had never heard of those last three artists.

Like most art lovers I was very familiar with O'Keeffe's sensuous blossoms and spare desert paintings, but what made me determined to see this exhibit was the description of Agnes Pelton's work: "Visionary paintings inspired by nature and theosophy, a religious philosophy based on universal connections."

"Visionary Art." I am drawn to that metaphysically imaginative genre because I find it so intriguing and mind-expanding. On my walls at home I have a mystically beautiful lithograph entitled *Astral Circus,* by visionary artist Bob Venosa, who studied with Salvador Dali, and another lithograph entitled *Sacred Ground,* by camouflage-style artist Bev Doolittle.

I was eager to view Pelton's work.

I invited my friend Diane, a fellow art lover and dabbler, to meet me the next day at 10:00 AM at the museum box office. She and I would have lunch after our tour.

The O.C. Museum of Art, which features contemporary art, is small compared to major galleries in Los Angeles, but the floor plan of its modern building is laid out in a most inviting way. There were quite a few visitors for a Wednesday but the open layout helped spread the crowd throughout the four main viewing galleries and small video screening rooms.

Upon entering the museum there is a foyer where—for this exhibit—information about the four artists, including biographies and photos, was displayed high and low on the walls and greatly enlarged for easy reading. Diane and I were eager to see the artists' paintings, so we went straight away into Gallery I where O'Keeffe's work was featured.

Diane took her time perusing the large array of imaginative watercolors and oils by the famous O'Keeffe. Though many of her paintings were familiar—the oversized and sensuous flowers, the bone-white skull of a long-horned steer—it was a thrill to see the originals in person.

I learned that O'Keeffe had also painted scenes in Hawaii and some of them were included in this exhibit. It was interesting, of course, but I soon left Diane with O'Keeffe because Agnes Pelton's creations were calling me.

I moved into Gallery II where the walls were devoted to Pelton's unique collection. Her paintings from the early 1900s, a few small landscapes and other more traditional paintings influenced by classicism and romanticism, were displayed in a small antechamber. Beyond it was the large main room of Gallery II.

On *those* vast walls were a multitude of Pelton's visionary abstractions in vibrant colors: large canvases and small—some pastels, but mostly oils. These imaginatively mystical paintings, so ahead of their time, dated from the early 1920s to the time of Pelton's death in 1961. Some of her pieces were accompanied by poems she had written about them. Each mounted poem was affixed to the wall next to its painting.

As I studied her paintings and read her poetry, I could see that Agnes Pelton's work flowed from the deep well of her soul and her own evolving spiritual journey, which was much like my own. It seemed as though she was speaking directly to me through her art—and I *knew* her.

Moving from painting to painting, carefully studying each one and allowing its message to impact me, I had a spontaneous emotional response that was overwhelming—and surprising.

Just as many people are, I am deeply moved by beauty, be it a gorgeous sunset or the strains of beautiful music.

A few years ago I treated myself to a front-and-center seat for an evening performance of *Swan Lake* presented by the famous Mariinsky ballet company. As the orchestra played Tchaikovsky's haunting "White Swan" theme, the prima ballerina dancing the part of Odette, the enchanted Swan Queen, performed so gracefully, so exquisitely, that her solos en pointe brought tears to my eyes as I sat there in the dark.

My emotional reaction in the art gallery that day came from the core of my being and I was so deeply touched by Agnes Pelton's creations and their silent messages to me, it wasn't just that my eyes got teary—I actually began sobbing uncontrollably.

I stifled my sobs as best I could because, after all, I was in this public place with my friend not far away and many other people now filling this gallery. I was embarrassed but I just couldn't stop crying. By this time Diane was near me, so I mentioned to her that I was moved to tears by Pelton's work (in case she was wondering about all the tissues and stifled sobs).

She just said, "That's great."

The depth of this profoundly personal and emotional encounter was like nothing I had ever before experienced. I sensed a connection to Agnes Pelton—an emotional connection and a *knowing* of who she was as a person and as a spiritual being.

While Diane visited the other galleries to view the works of the last two artists, I went back to the foyer to read everything about Pelton. A photograph of a handsome woman in her sixties was mounted on the upper wall next to Pelton's biography.

Among many other things I learned as I read her bio, was that in 1931 Agnes Pelton, at the age of fifty, had moved to Cathedral City, a small desert town on the outskirts of Palm Springs, California. There she lived alone in her modest cottage-studio, continuing as a prolific artist until 1961, when a serious fall ended her career—and her life soon after.

Agnes was eighty years old when she died.

Agnes Pelton's final and unfinished painting is titled: Light Center. The image—an elongated sphere of light—and this comment that Pelton made about it, reveal the spiritual truth she had embraced by the end of her life's journey: "Life is really all light, you know."

Light Center,
oil by Agnes Pelton (1961)

As I was reading these things about Pelton posted on the foyer wall, I remembered road trips with my parents and seeing the sign for the Cathedral City turnoff as we sped south on a highway through the desert. I recalled water-ski trips taken in my early twenties when I read that same sign on the way to the Salton Sea. All the while, Agnes Pelton was living right there as I passed by.

(I feel her energetic presence now as I am writing this.)

As soon as I got home from the museum and my lunch with Diane, I began searching the internet for any information I could find about Agnes Pelton. I spent hours online trying to discover everything about her and to locate copies of her paintings just so I could have them and study them. I found many sites displaying Pelton's paintings and lots of material about her—she has quite a following of collectors and fans who also love her work—but I was unable to find any of her poetry online.

Two days after my first visit, I returned to the museum box office and asked if I might go inside just to write down her poems.

"Of course," was the reply.

With yellow legal pad and pen in hand, I did just that, carefully notating the title of each poem's corresponding painting. I also made notes about who owned some of the paintings donated for this exhibit.

From my online research I learned that Agnes had not left a will when she died. Such a free spirit, I thought.

Agnes had many friends but few living relatives, so her unspoken-for works were eventually dispersed to different recipients. Many were art museums. Her private letters and other papers were donated to the Archives of American Art at the Smithsonian Institution.

Thanks to the internet, I found quite a few copies of her paintings, which I saved on my computer for my own enjoyment.

For several weeks, I continued to spend long days on my computer researching everything possible about Agnes Pelton—so focused, focused, focused on her paintings and poems and numerous articles about her, was I.

Oh yes, I definitely was obsessed with Agnes Pelton. And that was so contrary to my basic nature. Never before or since have I ever been so obsessive a follower or fan of anyone or anything.

With their permission, I was allowed online access to her private papers in the Smithsonian Archives. One thing I read from the Archives was a lengthy article that contained intimate, heartfelt details that Agnes had written in letters to her friends. There were other insightful revelations about her—and her unique spiritual journey—provided in various interviews she'd given.

I felt such a kinship with this woman—with this wonderful spiritual being—for we were alike in many ways.

She was an independent spirit who, at the age of fifty, began shifting her own spiritual and creative journey in a new direction, just as I had at that age. An aversion to allopathic medicine is another thing we have in common. It seemed as though we—each in our own time and space—were forging similar paths across an open field of self-discovery.

On my computer every day with such intense focus, I soon began to sense another's energies resonating with my own. It is a familiar sensation that I often experience and recognize as the presence of a being who wishes to communicate with me.

I sensed that these palpable energies (which I physically feel as a heaviness, a pressure around me) signaled the presence of the spiritual being that once inhabited the lifetime called "Agnes Pelton." I felt their presence—strong and powerful. Now as I write this, I feel it again.

The first time I sensed this one's presence seeking to communicate with me, I did a blending by simply opening myself to receiving and integrating their energies with mine. That was something I had learned to do long ago in channeling classes and had facilitated with much practice and with new techniques since then. The first blending began with some hesitation as my insecure self asked, "Is this really them or my imagination?"

This is what I experienced in two blendings:

I invited my Agnes being-friend's energies to be integrated with my own and I received this intuitive communication: "We see your light." Then a few days later, in a second blending: "We are twin lights who recognize each other."

Once again, my skeptical self warned, "Uh oh, this sounds like that new age 'twin flames' stuff." Then I suspected that *that* voice was really my negative ego spinning the message.

I knew that a reliable way to connect with this unseen being—this one I just knew was a friend—in a way that would transcend my limited-self's interference, was to do a self-guided meditation.

As I thought about the meditation, I recalled an aerial photo of a crop circle which had manifested in a field in Switzerland. I had seen it recently on a website devoted to crop circle sightings. It was first reported there on July 12, 2009. It was a huge design resembling a twisting ladder-like double helix.

Swiss double helix crop circle (2009)
Photographer: Flickr/Kecko

I sensed that this three-dimensional physical design that appeared in a wheat field was a *footprint* of the multi-dimensional energies that reflected my inter-twining connection to my being-friend once known as Agnes.

The double-helix crop design was the setting of our meeting-place in this first meditation:

As usual, I began my meditation by counting down from seven to one, taking my consciousness deeper and deeper—through my subconscious as the numbers got smaller—then deeper still into the unconscious realm. At number one, I sensed myself in my familiar safe place—sensing the colors, aromas, sounds and touch that make my safe place real.

Once there, I called upon my soul and higher self to transport me to an etheric double-helix crop design—a multi-dimensional version of the one in the physical realm. I soon found myself standing before a huge sphere of brilliant white light. I paused for a moment, and then stepped into the light. It was alive with powerful electro-magnetic energies, twisting, swirling, and lifting around me.

I invited my Agnes friend to join me. When I sensed their presence, I asked what their name was—how to refer to them in this dimension far beyond the physical realm. I sensed them as a feminine being and the name I heard was "Arianne."

After I concluded the meditation, I had a lot to digest.

In this second meditation, I went even deeper into the multi-dimensional unconscious and had a more full-on experience with Arianne/Agnes:

In a beautiful meadow-like setting, bordered on the left by a stand of trees, there Arianne and I both are. She communicates to me that she and I are friends beyond the physical realm and we help each other understand what each physical lifetime is about—the meanings behind the issues and challenges we face and our relationships with significant others. We help each other get insights from which to learn more about ourselves, thus evolving our spiritual growth.

I mentally ask, "Since we help each other here (on this plane), is she available to help me as I am making my way in my physical life?" I sense an affirmation.

I ask if she has any suggestions or insights about this stage of my journey in my Patty Paul life. Her suggestion is this: "Practice more proactive creation and less passive creation."

I understand what that means: Take responsibility for creating my reality before it manifests in my life.

In this sacred space, I notice a group of others nearby, and the understanding that comes to me is that we are a community of friends who come together to help each other—and also simply because we enjoy each other's company. Our gatherings are much like those with my physical metaphysician-friends when we attend the same workshops and social events, except that in this community we meet on a different plane of reality.

With all the past month's new experiences to share, and questions to ask about them, I could hardly wait until my next consultation on August 4th with my wise being-friend Elanor, channeled by Steve—another longtime friend and fellow metaphysician.

The day finally arrived and there I was in Steve's condo sitting on the couch across from Steve in his armchair. Elanor was now present and inhabiting Steve's physical body, via his channeling process. My tape recorder was on and I was eager to get Elanor's insights and suggestions regarding my latest adventures as Patty Paul.

I spoke to Elanor about the meaningful things that had happened during July and my emotional responses to them: my reaction to Agnes Pelton's work displayed in the museum, my strong sense of knowing her, my obsessive search for information about her, and my blendings and meditations with that spiritual being—especially my meditation the day before.

I asked for their insights about yesterday's meditation and the double helix crop design. Elanor suggested that I think of the pattern more as nautilus-like—a three-dimensional slice of a multi-dimensional nautilus chamber.

I asked if the name I had heard as "Arianne" was correct.

"Close enough," was Elanor's reply.

As I write this, however, I will continue to use "Agnes" for clarity's sake.

Elanor confirmed that Agnes and I not only *know* each other, we two beings have a long-standing and unique connection that includes an agreement once made between us. When I learned the details, I was amazed. Never before had I heard of such an arrangement.

As Elanor explained it, Agnes and I have a strong soul connection. We have lifetimes in Sirius together as friends and we very consciously chose to come here to planet Earth to do our consciousness-evolving work together.

Just like the nautilus design, there are these orbiting spirals and parallels and intersections that represent our many individual lifetimes—separate yet always connected.

I learned that Agnes and I have many lifetimes where we are alive either at the same time or close to the same time. Not always do we meet each other or know of each other—although there are some powerful lifetimes where we do so—but in that sort of spirally, double helix thread-like way, exists our definite soul-connection. Not to think of it as "twin souls," because that term is not accurate. We are basically just committed friends.

Regarding the group of others that I had seen in that final meditation, Elanor confirmed that there is a Sirius community and we do hang out together. It is a spiritual community originating in the Sirius star system, which also extends beyond our lifetimes there.

A group of us with spiritual connections—many of whom are currently powerful metaphysicians now in the physical world—come together on multi-dimensional planes. Often at these gatherings multiple sets of spiritual communities show up, including those from Lemuria and Atlantis.

Again, this is not about "soul mates" in that romantic New Age-consensus definition, it is the deeper truth of what is *behind* the term soul mates, i.e., certain souls just like each other and want to hang out together—hang out with their mates. Consequently, they literally plan to have some lifetimes at the same time and space where crisscrossing of paths may take place.

I wondered aloud if Agnes and I also had agreed to complete our physical lifetimes here on planet Earth at the same time.

"Could be," said Elanor, with a reminder that everything is always a matter of choice.

Elanor went into more detail about a significant lifetime that Agnes and I had together. "There is a Lemurian lifetime that is extremely deep and rich and powerful for the two of you."

This is what I learned from Elanor about that Lemurian lifetime, which I refer to in past tense, although it is happening now within a different dimension of the unconscious realm:

It seems that not only were we alive at the same time and knew each other, we were both women who were deeply and intensely in love and we lived together for our entire lives.

Our relationship began when we met in one of the Lemurian crystal cities; sacred centers devoted to teaching, healing, and personal and spiritual growth. I was teaching art there—in fact, teaching *visionary* painting—and she came to my class as a student.

Initially she had some rich talent, but as her teacher I was able to give her the multi-dimensional element that really enhanced her work.

(In Agnes Pelton's paintings that I viewed in the gallery, I sensed there was so much more going on than what appears on the canvas. It is a glimpse of the *bigger picture* of reality from a metaphysical perspective. That is what I was able to bring out in her as my student in Lemuria. That multi-dimensional element is what I recognized in her artwork that day at the gallery.)

In that ancient Lemurian land and lifetime, Agnes and I fell deeply in love. We lived together as a committed couple for the rest of our lives, just playing and creating together. We were a tremendous inspiration to everyone around us. They were in awe of the deep level of connection between the two of us.

I knew that it was my sensing of our deep connection that stirred within me as I studied Agnes Pelton's paintings and poetry that day at the gallery. I intuitively recognized her through her visionary art, and within me I felt the silent echoes of our timeless and wondrous love.

I learned that Agnes and I had pre-arranged to have many lifetimes where we will occasionally come into each other's sphere of influence— not always that we know each other personally but always there is a recognition—sometimes as fleeting as passing on the subway and we look at each other and sense something familiar. Perhaps a glance, a smile and we go on our way, for we have our own lives to live. There are also other lifetimes with a bit more interaction.

In the end, it is the deep love and beauty of our friendship and our commitment to each other that endures beyond time and space.

—and I thought I was simply going to an art exhibit that day!

Chapter 10

Gavriil

c. AD 50

Ancient Greece; Early Christianity

There was a time when I had a serious conflict with—and a lot of hostility toward—a man named Bob (not a relative or close acquaintance) who had power over a situation I was concerned about involving the living arrangements for a child. At least I believed I was powerless against his authority to make all decisions in the matter.

As a metaphysician who knows that I create my own reality, eventually I admitted to myself that I had put myself on that game board with Bob, and it was time to get off.

With some honest introspection, I owned that I was telling myself a story I had made up in my head: "Bob is in control and I'm not." I saw how I was giving my power away to him with that attitude.

I followed up my new insights with my usual meditative process, which included acknowledging and expressing the anger and resentment toward Bob that I had been harboring for weeks, and then letting it go. In one meditation I even beat him up! During my process I sensed that he too was conflicted about what was best for the child.

Despite doing that transformational process, which is usually so effective, my turmoil was still churning inside of me, keeping me awake night after night. I knew in my gut that it had to do with my ongoing rage at the basic premise of male chauvinism: Men are superior and therefore in charge, and women are subservient. That conflict between male and female, so familiar to me, was present in many of my lifetimes.

Through the years, I have dealt with this issue many times, in different ways. One reason I chose to be a woman in this lifetime was to have more opportunities to feel and release my latent rage and resentment around this male vs. female issue.

I knew that by recognizing the beliefs and attitudes I was holding onto, acknowledging my inner thoughts and feelings—then owning the choices and decisions I had been making, I would eventually be set free to move on.

But now, I clearly needed to get some deeper insights and guidance about this problem from my wise friend Elanor, at my upcoming consultation.

When I described my conflict and anger with Bob, Elanor said it was *my own* inner male chauvinist who wants to do battle with him.

I got it right away. Domineering male chauvinist Bob was a reflection/projection of the same energies within multi-faceted me. Bob and I were resonating with the same vibrational frequencies, producing a magnetic field that was drawing us together.

I reminded myself that it's never about *them*; it's always about *me* creating my own reality. Time to take back my power.

When I got home from my consultation, I thought about my inner turmoil. Its persistence indicated to me that I have other lifetimes resonating with the same energies and seeking my attention. My sleepless nights were caused by that "static interference" which kept me going over and over this problem, unable to let it go. To have peace, I knew that I needed to discover and understand one or more of those related lifetimes by visiting it in a few self-guided meditations.

In this first meditation I met Gavriil:

Guiding myself deeply into my unconscious, I find myself in my beautiful safe place on the shores of a turquoise lagoon. I invite my soul to join me where I stand on the warm, white sand. In personified form, they enter my space and come beside me. I feel their loving energy as we embrace. I ask my soul to help me connect with a lifetime having inner conflicts like my own.

I sense my soul's arms around me as I lay my head on their shoulder, surrendering to a feeling of powerlessness. With my eyes closed, I am lifted into the ethers, wafting this way and that through multi-dimensions of consciousness. Eventually I sense myself gently descending until my feet touch solid ground.

My eyes open and I find myself inside a sacred place I know well, a place where I have met several other of my lifetimes in transcendent meditations. I know it as "the Lemurian healing chamber," a large circular room with a domed ceiling. There is a feeling of reverence here.

The far end of the space, to my left, is dimly lit. At my end of the room, on my right there are several tiers of cement-gray stadium seating curved in a semi-circle. The lighting is brighter overhead, though I see no source. I take a seat on a lower tier and sense that my higher self and my soul are sitting with me.

I call forth one who is caught up in a conflict with male chauvinism.

From the rear of the chamber, a male figure comes forward and stands before us. I thank him for coming and ask his name. It sounds like "Gabriel." (I later learn it is actually Gavriil.) I also hear the unspoken words: "fisher of men." I wonder if this lifetime is about Jesus or the disciples, then I realize that that voice is my negative ego trying to distract me. I ignore it.

Gavriil is dressed in the garb of the times and the setting, which I sense to be during the early rise of Christianity in Ancient Greece around AD 50. He wears plain robes in a soft fabric, light in color. He seems to be in his thirties.

I invite him to tell me what is troubling him and to share his feelings.

I learn that Gavriil, who has an air of maturity, is a teacher of philosophy. He is conflicted because he knows that men and women are equals and that their value as human beings and spiritual beings is the same. But the emerging Christianity is founded upon the assumption of male superiority and female subservience. If Gavriil doesn't join with the local Christian zealots by promoting their rigid beliefs, he will be seen as an enemy and punished—ostracized, or perhaps worse.

(I feel his inner turmoil and sense of helplessness resonating with my own.)

To conclude this time together, I thank him for sharing and I and my unseen friends surround Gavriil, filling him with light and love. Gavriil turns to his left and departs.

To better understand the context of Gavriil's lifetime, I did some research and learned that in AD 50, Athens was under Roman rule. Apostle Paul had journeyed to Athens in that year as a missionary proselytizing Christianity, a new religion that would be deemed a threat to the status quo.

The inevitable clash of their respective ideologies would eventually lead to violence between avid neo-Christians who believed in their one true Father-God, and the majority of citizens, who adhered to the prevailing Greco-Roman polytheistic belief system and its multitude of gods and goddesses.

In my next meditation a few days later, I visited Gavriil's lifetime as an observer. In the account that follows, I have supplemented my experience of his lifetime with a few other details my research provided, including specific subjects taught by philosophy teachers in those days, so as to have a more comprehensive understanding of his situation. This is what I discovered about Gavriil's life and times:

Gavriil teaches philosophy to the sons of wealthy families at a prominent school in Athens. As the son of a prosperous merchant, Gavriil received a fine education—heavily influenced by Plato's metaphysical themes. He is well-prepared for his prestigious position, and well respected.

More valuable than his education, however, is Gavriil's innate wisdom. He stands out in his world of academia as a man of letters with a soul,

Gavriil is a philosophy teacher who respects his students; he shares with them what he holds to be true about various subjects including mathematics, logic, ethics, astronomy, rhetoric, and of course metaphysics.

As a more enlightened individual, Gavriil inherently knows that women and men are equals. Neither sex is superior nor inferior to the other. He knows that men and women have the same worth and they are deserving of *equal* acceptance and respect. Those higher truths are what he always presents to his students.

The subjects he teaches help his students make sense of the world in a non-religious way. Ultimately, Gavriil encourages each student to make up their own mind about what to believe based upon what rings true for them personally. For those very reasons Gavriil is now being closely monitored. His enlightened world view is the crux of the problem that now threatens his life.

The emerging Christian belief-system is based upon a two-fold mind-set: patriarchy that establishes male authority—with its ultimate expression, a Father-God as Supreme Being—and the male-chauvinistic concept that men are inherently superior to women in every way. Women are deemed to be less spiritually evolved—truly lesser beings meant to be subservient to men. Members of a small cabal of Christian zealots in Athens hold Christian dogma as The One and Only Truth, and those who contradict it must be silenced.

The cabal's members use bullying tactics to ferret out and punish those they deem to be heretics, targeting teachers in particular because of their ability to influence others.

Knowing he is being watched and that his life is in danger, Gavriil is torn. To avoid being targeted by the Christian zealots he must no longer teach subjects and ideas that are contrary to their rigid beliefs. In particular, he must stop speaking to his students about the equality of men and women. As an ethical person who values honesty above all, how can he compromise his integrity in that way? He believes that although he is right, he is powerless against outside forces. (I can relate to that situation.)

It has been a while since I first met Gavriil in meditation. For some unknown reason, I have avoided exploring Gavriil's life as participant, avoided actually being Gavriil and experiencing whatever he is going through. For days I've felt an inner resistance to doing that important meditation, but this morning I finally bit the bullet.

What happens to Gavriil—what happens to *us*—is not what I anticipated. It is shocking.

This is my experience as participant—actually being Gavriil—after I am transported by my soul to Gavriil's lifetime:

I see Gavriil sitting on a bench in the courtyard of his home. Consciously blending my energies with his, we become one.

We hold our lowered head in our hands, feeling despair and hopelessness. Such sorrow fills our heart and our tears begin to flow.

Our thoughts cannot find a path out of this impossible dilemma. We love and respect our students and must continue to offer them our highest truths, as we always have. And yet doing so may end in violence, a danger for us all.

Perhaps we should abandon this life we have in Athens. Go where there is peace for us. Yet that seems the coward's way. No, we must do the honorable thing—but what is it? And how do we survive?

We arise and leave the courtyard through a heavy wooden gate to the street. We walk alongside the busy city street, heading nowhere in particular—just walking to clear our thoughts.

Suddenly we are set upon by four young men who charge out of an alleyway. They are shouting angry words: "Heretic! Idol worshiper!" We are shocked and frozen in fear. We feel their knives stabbing, stabbing into our flesh. We fall to the ground, our blood flowing around us. "So this is how it ends." –our final thought.

When I come out of this meditation, I feel stunned. I had no idea this tragic end would be part of Gavriil's life story. As I write this, I still feel a heaviness, like a dense cloud cocooning me. I know I will visit Gavriil again, for there is energy-shifting and lifting to be done.

A few days before I did my final mediation, I found out how extremely important that lifting of Gavriil's influence is for my current lifetime—and for all of my lifetimes—at my next consultation with Elanor.

I learned that in those last seconds after he was stabbed but still alive, Gavriil drew certain conclusions about "the big event" (the Christian zealots stabbing him to death) and made some profound decisions that were stored in our unconscious.

Elanor suggested that I visit Gavriil at the time of his death to learn what those conclusions and decisions were in order to understand their influence on my life now.

This is what transpired in my last time with Gavriil:

I am with Gavriil, who is lying in the street in a bloody pool, just after his death. I lift his light-body from the physical one now lifeless, and I tell him: "I come as a friend to talk with you. Your life is over now. What conclusions did you draw in those last seconds after the event that ended your life in such a brutal way? What decisions did you make in those final moments?

Gavriil replies: "Christianity is bad. Violent. Those who believe in it must be educated. They must change. They must be told about the equality between men and women. The violence must end. This transgression must not happen again."

"What is the transgression you refer to?"

"Violence arising from ignorance."

"How do you believe it will be ended?"

"They must be taught higher truths."

I thank this one and lifting their light body from the empty shell, I integrate their energies into the greater being that we are.

Before leaving the meditation, I heard this unspoken vow: "I will fight this forever!"

Now I understand why it was so important for me to learn what conclusions were drawn and what hard-core decisions were made in Gavriil's final moments, for they were infused with the powerful emotions he felt in those last seconds—the shock, the rage and the despair. Those emotions gave his conclusions and decisions substance. Solidity. That heavy cloud hangs over all my lifetimes.

My spiritual journey in this Patty Paul lifetime has meant growing and changing and becoming more by constantly letting go of old beliefs and opening to new, less inhibiting beliefs.

Back in 1985, when I made the choices to change and to discover more of my spiritual nature, I immediately began learning wonderful metaphysical truths about how and why I create my own reality—all of it—all of the time.

Not only did I gain valuable information and techniques, I digested them and began living my life based upon what I was learning. Right away everything began changing for me in positive ways. Miracles and real magic were happening in my life. So much fun!

"Wow," I thought. "Everyone should know about this!" I had the urge to grab people by their lapels and share this amazing news about how *they* create *their* own reality. (I am sure that many feel the same way about their own convictions.)

Around 1988, I began writing articles and giving talks—lots of them— on many subjects related to personal empowerment and spiritual growth. I loved doing those things, especially talking with people and answering their questions. What I shared was quite well-received.

In 1995, my book *A New Spirituality: Beyond Religion* was published. My book found favor with many readers and reviewers, and I made author appearances at numerous bookstores during the next few years. That felt so right for me at the time.

Because I have continued to grow and change, replacing old beliefs with new ones, I now have a much different perspective. I relate to my personal reality—*the little picture*—and the reality playing out on the world stage—*the big picture*—far differently than I used to.

Rather than feeling the need—or responsibility—to teach, enlighten, or change (aka *fix*) others, I endeavor to accept and respect them just as they are. For I know that everyone is on their own soul's journey and I have no idea what someone else's might be.

I now *get* that I am only responsible for my own growth and change. If I inspire others by *showing* who I am as a person living my truth, rather than telling them what to do—that is personally gratifying.

And yet I still have these two persistent inner voices:

The Teacher—who chatters away in my head as though giving a lecture for the purpose of "enlightening" others (Read: disabusing them of their "faulty" beliefs), and its cousin The Reformer, who is triggered by the prevalence of male chauvinism in our so-called "man's world," and the patriarchal religions it created—especially Christian religions.

It often takes a while, but when I finally acknowledge the inner chatter of The Teacher or The Reformer, I end their static by consciously choosing to silence them, then choosing to be *present*—in the moment—as my truer self. Then I open myself to receiving from expanded levels of multi-dimensional consciousness. In short: Show up. Shut up. Open up to receiving.

I can see how the influence of Gavriil's lifetime, with his rock-solid conclusions and decisions about male chauvinism and Christianity, keeps The Reformer at the ready. More importantly, I see that I unconsciously have been engaging in a never-ending battle with male chauvinism—and with those who subscribe to the religions it created. So exhausting!

I cannot change the Gavriil lifetime. It is what it is. But knowing what strong conclusions and decisions were made in it has helped to lift its heavy influence from my life.

What a relief!

Chapter 11

Eriken

Atlantis, 2nd Civilization

This is the story of Eriken, whose lifetime takes place near the end-times of the second civilization of Atlantis. It is the lifetime of one who could be seen as a lesser self. Not bad or wrong, just one with limited possibilities for success and happiness. I chose to experience such a lifetime to help me be more compassionate and understanding and less judgmental of those who are constricted in similar ways.

Deep down I had always judged harshly such lesser lifetimes—my own and others'—deeming them to be a shameful waste. Something to be overcome and forgotten. That judgment has also applied to earlier periods in my current life about which I harbored secret shame.

In my first meditation, with my soul's guidance I was transported to the familiar sacred space where I often meet my other lifetimes. It is a large clearing in a forest with a magnificent bonfire ablaze in the center—its orange flames leaping and sparking towards the night sky. The surrounding trees reflecting its glow. This is what transpired:

> I and my soul sit on a log facing the fire. Upon my invitation, one slowly shuffles forth from behind the bonfire. He is a stoop-shouldered man with an aura of sadness and defeat. I ask his name. "Eriken," he replies.

I learn that this sorry being lives a derelict existence near the end-times of the second civilization of Atlantis.

I sense he is addicted to drugs, or perhaps alcohol, which help him escape his painful life, and soon will bring an end to it.

With Eriken before me, I thank him for his presence and tell him I wish to experience his reality—to really get to know and understand him.

What follows are the powerful, life changing truths I discover as I explore Eriken's world in my next meditation:

Now present in Eriken's reality, I find myself walking down a back alley filled with garbage and overflowing trash bins—large carts made of a thick, woven rattan-like material affixed on four sides to a sturdy wooden frame. Some containers have lids covering the rubbish, but most do not.

As I open to the sights and sounds and smells here, I come upon a man sitting on the filthy ground next to one of the open trash carts. He is dressed in rags, certainly not enough to keep him warm on this chilly morning. His emaciated body is covered in dirt and sores. He appears to be in his twenties, though he is so dissipated it is hard to tell.

I crouch down in front of him and when his eyes meet mine, I tell him that I come as a friend to get to know him. To learn how he came to be here and what it is like for him living in this way. What his thoughts and feelings are.

I learn that Eriken was born into deep poverty and like everyone else who had been, he is an outcast. Worthless like the trash in this alley.

At this time in Atlantis, those living in poverty are deemed undesirable by the government because they don't mesh with the fabric of Atlantis' mainstream "respectable and productive" citizenry.

The government and the majority who support it, choose to ignore the outliers. "Castaways" is the label applied to all who are deemed too different to be accepted. Castaways are not only the poor and homeless, they are also the mentally ill, and all non-conformists—anyone who does not hold the same values and beliefs as the consensus.

(Because I wanted to truly experience *being* Eriken, I used my *uncommon senses* to blend his energies with mine: I open myself to sensing and integrating his *substance*, his *light*, his *warmth*, his *movement* and his *voice*. I draw in and physically feel these vibrational frequencies blending with my own.)

Now at one with Eriken, I feel him. I am filled with sorrow and self-disgust. I hate myself and I want my miserable life to end. I am alone in this world. I always have been. I don't belong. Never have I fit in anywhere. This is what I deserve. There is something bad and wrong about me and I can't fix it. I don't even know what it is. Now I don't care anymore.

Death is my only escape. When I die, who I am will be over, done. I am fearful about that—and part of me clings to this miserable life. I dread the inevitable but I have no more chances. No more hope. Soon I will be extinguished and who I am will disappear into the dark abyss of nothingness.

(I consciously withdraw my energies from Eriken's to engage him objectively once more.)

I tell him that I now understand what he thinks and feels about himself and about his lot in life—but a higher truth is that he is lovable and loved just as he is. That he is so much more than this one life he is living.

I embrace Eriken and fill him with a *sense of being safe and secure*, and with a *sense of having value*—inherent worth equal to all others'—simply because he exists. I fill him with a *sense of being loved unconditionally*, and with a *sense of having unlimited access to all knowledge and wisdom*. I fill him with a *sense of his inherent beauty*, and his *spiritual oneness with the divine creator of all that is*.

Then I integrate this one into the more—the multi-faceted, multi-dimensional wholeness where *I* becomes *we* as the greater being we are.

The elegant thing about this work is that it creates a positive rippling effect that instantly impacts all of my lifetimes—most of them lost and forgotten. They are spontaneously reclaimed and integrated into the whole—our united states of being. And that accelerates my spiritual journey by quantum leaps!

Chapter 12

Erin-Bridget

c. 1400

Norman Ireland

Some years ago, an acquaintance of mine named Amy, who lived in Northern California, phoned me to ask if she could stay at my house in Orange County while she took care of some business here. "Sure," I replied. I only knew Amy from conversations we'd had at some of the metaphysical workshops we'd both been attending through the years, but I was looking forward to her visit.

At one point during her short stay, Amy confided to me that she had been told, by those who made such decisions, that she could no longer attend the metaphysical workshops that meant so much to her, because of something she had said or done that they found offensive. I had never heard of that happening before.

Amy was devastated and I really felt for her. Just imagining being banished like that stirred up my childhood fears about rejection and not belonging.

Soon after Amy's visit, I heard about someone I had once met who was being shunned by their fellow church members. I thought to myself, "Shunned? Who gets shunned in this day and age? Hmmm—these rare happenings seem to be waving a flag to get my attention."

Then I recalled being blackballed from joining a private sorority by two of my high school "friends" who decided they didn't like me anymore. It hurt at the time, which was my junior year way back in 1953.

More recently, after spending the day with a group of metaphysical friends, my old insecure-self whispered in my ear: "They're probably going out to dinner together—and they didn't invite you." Being older and wiser, I immediately said "shut up" to that subconscious storyteller.

Since whispers about not belonging were getting louder and closer to home, I sensed there was a lifetime or two with the same issues, clamoring for attention. Clearly it was time to visit a lifetime experiencing painful feelings of rejection and isolation.

In my first meditation, I met Erin-Bridget, a young girl gifted with psychic powers, who lives in Ireland when it is under English rule (the Norman Ireland era in the 1400's). This was my experience being with her:

Upon meeting Erin-Bridget, I tell her that I am a visitor from far away and that I would like to get to know her and to hear about her life. I want to be her friend. "Maybe we can help each other," I say. She smiles.

I find that she is a loving and open young girl known for her psychic powers and talent in the healing arts. She has a sadness, a loneliness about her, for she has no close friends—so different is she from other people. Even her family alienates her. Her Ma thinks she is odd. Her Da forbids any talk about her visions. Their criticism hurts her—and I feel a pang of her pain. Erin-Bridget's grandmother was her only ally, but now she is dead.

As I walk by her side through the village, I see that she is friendly to all. Children flock to her as she strolls through the village. She carries sweets in her pockets and potions in a pouch for skinned knees and the like.

I learn that many villagers not only come to her for her herbs and potions, many—especially the women—seek her intuitive insights about their lives.

On our walk, I notice two women whispering to each other as we pass by. Erin-Bridget says she recently told them that their husbands had visited a certain woman who lives on the outskirts of the village.

Before we finish this time together, we go on a picnic near a lake. We eat bread and cheese and drink water from a nearby spring. I say that I appreciate her gift as a seer and ask if she sees anything about my life? She says she sees me speaking to a large number of people—"But they are invisible to you."

Erin-Bridget's comment did not make sense to me when I did that meditation in 2003. It does now, because in 2015 I uploaded fifty-seven videos of my TV talk show, "Living Wisdom with Patty Paul," to YouTube. The "invisible" viewers are in countries around the world.

In a more recent visit to Erin-Bridget, this is what transpires:
Some time has gone by and Erin-Bridget tells me that things are worse for her now. Her father has built her a cabin in the woods where she lives by herself, shunned by her family.

(When she mentions the cabin, a vision appears to me: I see a pig lying on its left side with its throat slit below its right ear. I see the open wound and red blood around it. I sense it is her pet and someone has killed it, perhaps to threaten her.)

Once again, I speak to her about our being friends. Allies helping each other.

This time we go to a quiet place in a forest to talk. A beautiful waterfall is nearby. During our chat, I tell her of my aspirations to speak to a larger group of people (I was giving small workshops at the time) and I ask her what she sees for me. She says, "There is a trap set. You need to remove the trap." (Another puzzling comment.)

After that meditation, I was curious about the "trap set" remark so I sat on my couch and opened my consciousness to access my Erin-Bridget lifetime:
I sense that this life-changing event happened to her: She was invited to speak openly before a gathering of the villagers to tell them of her visions and prophecies. Then they used what she said against her, to ostracize her and to run her out of town.

That was the trap set for her.

My first meditational visits to Erin-Bridget's lifetime took place in 2003. I wrote summaries of what I experienced in them and saved them as Word documents, just as I have done for many of the lifetimes I have explored since 1985. I also have descriptions of my lifetimes on audio tapes recorded during consultations with Elanor and other wise friends. Somehow, I always knew that one day I would write a book about my other lifetimes.

Now it is mid-2019 and I am picking up the thread of Erin-Bridget's story as I write this chapter. I see that her warning—"There is a trap set. You need to remove the trap."—is still dangling in midair.

The synchronicity of writing this chapter and being reminded of Erin-Bridget's warning about the potential trap awaiting me is not lost on me. It seems like her message is meant for me right now because of where I am in my life—and in my relationship with this book.

It would be wise to find out what kind of "trap" is waiting for me.

Once again, after getting comfortably seated, I open myself to receiving knowledge from expanded levels of consciousness. These are the words that come to me:

> The trap is one I could set for myself. A way to pull the rug out
> from under manifesting success for my book by seeking outside
> approval—outside acceptance—and in that way, giving away my
> power to create my reality, to others. Giving away my authorship
> to outside authorities who will decide if my book is good enough.

I appreciated receiving that reminder to let go of my old limiting beliefs, fears, and self-doubts, as I go forward with my plans for this book.

Erin-Bridget's other curious message from a mediation long ago, about seeing me speaking to a large number of people who are invisible to me, also makes sense now. Through this book, I will be speaking to readers who are invisible to me.

The timeliness of Erin-Bridget's messages is an example of the living, breathing relationship I have with my other lifetimes as I write about them here.

Getting to know and understand those lifetimes by exploring them in meditations, helps me discover more of who I truly am as a multi-dimensional spiritual being—which is the whole purpose of my soul's journey—and the *true* success I have already gained from writing this book.

Chapter 13

Glimpses
from Other Lifetimes

Many times through the years, I have experienced visions suddenly appearing to my mental eyes—each one as clear as a photograph or film clip, and always out of context with what I was focused on in that moment. Most often it has happened during a guided meditation heading in an entirely different direction.

These spontaneous visions have always turned out to have great significance, for each one related to some issue in my current life. Often one I was unaware of even having.

What follows are a few of those mental snapshots and how each of them connects to this lifetime of mine.

Dying Alone:

When *The English Patient* was first released, I went to a matinee at a local theater with great anticipation. I had read the early reviews and knew this would be a good film, although I didn't yet know the storyline. I found that it unfolded in flashbacks as recalled by the title character, Almásy.

Sitting there in the darkened theater, I was engrossed in Almásy's fascinatingly complex story playing out on the big screen—that is until a tragedy involving his beloved Katherine was revealed. I was absolutely devastated by what happened to her. I felt the pain of it in the depth of my being. Mine was *not* a normal reaction.

To briefly summarize: Katherine was severely injured in a plane crash in the Libyan desert, where Almásy was awaiting her arrival. He pulled her from the wreckage and carried her to a nearby cave for shelter. He bound her broken ankle, built her a fire, and left her with a small kerosene lantern and his promise to return with help as soon as possible. He would have to hike through the desert to find that help. Unfortunately, the circumstances he encountered on that trek made it impossible for him to return in time to save her.

In Katherine's final scene in the cave, too much time has passed without food and water. The lantern's light dims and finally goes out. We know she will soon die. Alone, abandoned, in total darkness.

As I witnessed the hopelessness of her situation, I *felt* what that abandonment was like. I began quietly weeping, until I forced myself to stifle it. Most of the movie remained and I had to get through it. But I found it difficult to concentrate.

As soon as the film ended, I rushed to my car in the parking lot and sat in it for an hour sobbing my heart out. I knew my overreaction must be tied to another lifetime or two. But with my busy life, I put the matter on the back burner.

A couple of years later I learned why I had identified so strongly with Katherine's fate.

One afternoon during a weekend workshop given by a wise friend called Torah (no connection to the Hebrew text), along with the others there, I was intently following the meditational journey being guided by Torah. Suddenly—with no connection to our meditation—I saw with my mental eyes a tableau of a man lying on his right side in an open field dried yellow by the sun. He was leaning on his right elbow as he watched a small group of men in tattered military khakis walking farther and farther away from him. Then the vision disappeared.

When Torah's meditation was over, it was time to share our experiences. When my turn came, I asked for Torah's insights about the vision that had popped into my consciousness.

After a long pause, they said it was a lifetime of mine in which the badly wounded soldier, left to die alone on the battlefield, wondered if he was so worthless, if his life had so little meaning that his comrades could just walk away without even a backward glance. He died filled with despair. Torah added that this lifetime's painful influence hovers over my current life and suggested that I visit him in meditation to give him comfort and love as I hold him in my arms until he passes on.

I did exactly that a few days later and was filled with a great sense of peace.

A Feast of Falcons:
While doing a self-guided meditation to discover another lifetime where I am a writer, a vision suddenly appeared to my mental eyes and it seemed that I was drawn into it. This was my experience:

Silhouetted against a grey sky, I see a tall, dark-haired woman standing on a rugged slope of land overlooking the sea. She wears a long black cloak to protect against the harsh winds, as she looks out over the dark ocean far below. We seem to be somewhere on the northern coast of Britain. The timing is near the end of the eighteenth century.

This woman intrigues me. I sense that she visits this remote and rugged place to find peace and to collect her thoughts. As I near her, she turns toward me. I introduce myself and ask her name. "Winifred" is what I hear, then the phrase, "A feast of falcons."

At my next consultation with my wise friend Elanor, I asked about the woman I had envisioned on the rugged cliffs and the words I had heard. This is what Elanor told me about this lifetime of mine, and what I discovered in a subsequent meditation:

Winifred is courageous in both the way she lives her life and as a writer. She is an independent, freethinking woman and writes from that perspective. She is certainly ahead of her time in that regard. This is an era when Jane Austen's books are all the rage, and Winifred's published books are not popular. Many of her writings are never even published. Winifred cares little about that because she writes them as a creative expression of her own values and beliefs. Her own truth. She basically writes for herself. Her given name was Elizabeth, but she changed it to Winifred when she began writing.

A Feast of Falcons is the title of the book she is working on. It focuses on the plight of poor children toiling in factories owned by the barons of industry—the "falcons" who "feast" off their labors.

Winifred knows it is unlikely that she will find a publisher for her book, but she is a courageous and principled fighter for what is right.

I am inspired by my lifetime as Winifred.

A Human Child in the Faerie Realm:

Once again, an unexpected scene popped into my consciousness during a meditation, this one being led by a wise friend named Baratta. I was attending their afternoon workshop entitled "Crystal Gateways to the Faery Realm," with about eight other people.

The vision that suddenly appeared to me was of a little girl about five years old lying on her side in a fetal position upon a mossy forest floor. Her still body was being attended to with loving care and respect by a group of faeries, some of whom were tall and willowy. They were gently swaddling her body from head to feet with wide strips of soft cloth. Then the vision disappeared.

After the meditation, Baratta invited us to share our experiences. When my turn came, I described the scene I had envisioned and asked for their insights about its meaning. After a long pause, this is what Baratta said:

The little girl had wandered away from her home in a rural area—a farming community—and out of curiosity had entered the dense forest. Perhaps she was chasing an animal she had seen. The narrow path she followed led deeper and deeper into the forest until the path disappeared under tangled growth. She was now lost in the forest.

The child tried to find her way out, but soon became disoriented and very frightened. Alone deep in the forest for many days and nights without food or water, she often cried out in despair. By expressing her fear and anguish with such strong emotional energy, the veil between the human realm and the faerie realm was pierced.

The faeries had been aware of her presence in the forest and now they could interact with her in their domain. They were touched by her vulnerability, but it was too late to help her as she had already died from hunger and exposure. The faeries lovingly bound her small body and carried it out of the forest, then placed it where humans, perhaps her parents, could find it.

The little girl's is another lifetime of mine, and I loved hearing how the faeries had so tenderly cared for her, or rather—us.

Accelerated Journey Crystal:
In the early 1990s I attended a weekend workshop entitled "Your Accelerated Journey," conducted by a wise friend named Lazaris. There were several hundred of us seated in a hotel ballroom for this event.

Soon after the Saturday morning session began, Lazaris invited us to do a "blending" in which they would blend their energies with each of ours as we sat quietly with our eyes closed. During the blending Lazaris would speak aloud to the large group in attendance, and also psychically give personal messages to some individuals in the audience. I had been attending every Lazaris workshop since early 1986, so I was familiar with this intimate experience.

During prior blendings, sometimes Lazaris had spoken to me privately, but this time a startling image suddenly appeared to my mental eyes. It was *way* out of context with what Lazaris was saying to the group.

What I saw very clearly was a tall, slender shaft tapering toward its pointed tip and resembling—of all things—a phallus! What *is* that? thought I, in shock. The image remained for a few seconds, then—poof— it was gone. It took a minute for me to re-focus on what Lazaris was saying.

Our last day was Sunday and per tradition Lazaris would be handing each one of us a small crystal from a basket of them on a table near their chair. I took my place in one of the lines that curved around the room. Soon I stood in front of Lazaris and told them my name. Lazaris said something personal and meaningful to me as they put a crystal in my outstretched right hand.

Back in my chair I looked at the gift in my hand. It was a slender six-sided crystal tapering to a point at the top and almost two inches long. It looked just like the image I saw in the blending.

Soon after returning home I had a jeweler fashion my crystal as a pendant I could wear on a gold chain. I had him adorn the gold cap with a tiny cabochon emerald.

I treasure this gift from Lazaris—made more special because it was previewed for me in that blending, and because my dictionary told me "A phallus is used as a symbol of the generative power of nature." That symbolism made sense to me because my connection to nature is one of my seven focuses in this lifetime.

I *know* that I am on an accelerated spiritual journey and my crystal pendant is a treasured reminder.

Another Mother:

Soon after the death of an elderly friend named Mary, who had been more like a mother to me than my own all through my childhood, I was sitting before a wise friend named Ophelia, seeking their insights and guidance in our monthly consultation. At one point I asked if Mary had been my mother in another lifetime because we had had such a close lifelong relationship in this one.

As Ophelia was taking a long pause, suddenly I got a mental image of a little girl climbing on top of a large wooden table in the center of an old-fashioned kitchen. A woman—her mother—was rolling out dough on the tabletop. I felt the loving connection between mother and child. Then the vision vanished.

Ophelia said, "What was that?" They had sensed the energy-shift from my present lifetime to the one I had just tapped into.

Ophelia confirmed that the one who was Mary was also my loving mother in the other lifetime I had glimpsed. I know that she returned in my current lifetime to provide the love and affection I needed as little Patty.

Whenever I think of Mary, I am thankful for her presence in my childhood. I am also grateful for her daughter Marlene's lifelong friendship, which began when we met in kindergarten at five years of age—and has lasted all these years to the present time, as the eighty-somethings we are now.

Herren:

The subject of the Lazaris weekend I was attending was "Atlantis." It was the first of many about Atlantis and its three civilizations that would be offered in the next few years.

In one of our first meditations that weekend, Lazaris guided us to an unspecified locale in Atlantis. It might be a different place and experience for each of us and we were encouraged to pay attention to the details in our surroundings. The buildings, the people, how they were dressed—anything that caught our eye.

As Lazaris was suggesting things we might look for, in *my* meditation a man in dark colored robes came toward me as I strolled down a narrow cobblestone road leading to the center of town. I introduced myself as a visitor. His name was Herren.

By silent communication, I learned that Herren was a wise spiritual teacher called a priest—a title of respect—and that our meeting was important because Herren's inner masculine and feminine energies worked together in balance and harmony—a state of being I was meant to experience.

We merged our energies, and in that blending—for the first time—I felt what it is like to have my masculine and feminine energies resonating in balance and harmony. The closest description of how that felt is *centered, grounded,* and *empowered.*

I have found that the more I practice *being* in that state of balance and harmony, the easier it is to feel it.

Loves, Lost and Found—Completing the Stories

Chapter 14

Jim

I met Jim in December 1971, six months after my husband, Harry Paul, had perished in a plane crash. I was at a restaurant having holiday drinks with friends when Jim approached me and introduced himself. He and I ended up chatting for quite a while—long enough for me to see that we had things in common. And he was an attractive, intelligent, nice guy. Somehow, he learned what my phone number was—being in law enforcement, he had his ways—and he called me a few days later. Eventually I agreed to have dinner with him.

Before long we began an exclusive relationship. Things were moving fast, and I had not taken enough time to mourn my husband's death. My heart was still broken and sometimes I would just begin to weep quietly. But Jim was not put off by that—at least he didn't let on that he was. After about a year we got engaged. Diamond ring and all.

I bought a house in a good area for my teenage son and daughter to grow up in and Jim moved in with us. Our ordinary, domesticated life felt nice. Peaceful and secure. But after about a year and a half, I began having some personal misgivings about our future together. My intuition was whispering that marrying Jim was not the right thing for me. However, I didn't share my doubts with him.

My dilemma was soon resolved when Jim's employer transferred him to another county far from my house. Distance and time helped to end our marriage plans and un-prioritize our relationship.

That was part one of our relationship saga.

Part two began in December 1986.

I had been living and working in Jim's area since 1979, the year I purchased a residence there. One day during the Christmas season, I contacted Jim as a friend from his past. We met for drinks that evening and found we had much to catch up on. By that time, I was following my metaphysical path of personal growth and he was somewhat interested in metaphysics. We started dating casually and after a few months, I started thinking, "Hmmm—I wonder if there's a future here."

I had no idea what Jim was thinking.

As I was pondering the possibilities, I was fortunate to have been given a consultation with a wise friend from whom I was learning so much about *everything* in their many workshops I was attending.

Since my consultation took place while I was still seeing Jim, one of the things I asked was whether Jim and I have other lifetimes together. I learned that we do. At least four of them. I was told that two are rather repetitive, but the other two are significant because they greatly influence our relationship in this lifetime.

Our first lifetime together has a positive influence, the second is tragic. This is what I learned about my blissful lifetime with Jim:

This lifetime takes place in a rural area of Atlantis around 28,070 BC, near the end of its second civilization. I am the first-born child—a daughter—of a powerful landowner. My father is a land baron who owns hundreds of thousands of acres of highly productive land used for farming and the mining of fossil fuels. Though extremely wealthy and influential, he is quite a down-to-earth fellow.

Throughout childhood I am a rough and tumble tomboy growing up on our farm. But when adolescence hits, I must learn what it is to be a well-mannered lady. It is a big adjustment that I am not happy about. Unhappy, that is, until I meet Jim (keeping that name to avoid confusion). He's a young man my age hired on to work in the fields.

I am *very* interested in this handsome new field hand. The more I sneak peeks at him, the more I am physically attracted to him and his strong, well-built body. So physically attracted it is embarrassing.

One evening I go to the barn to turn in my horse at the end of the day and Jim is there. My heart stops. Here I am this wealthy, semi-sophisticated young woman, now practically falling apart, stumbling over my words as I try to speak to him. When he speaks to me it is very softly, and I discover, to my surprise, that he is kind and gentle as well as sexy.

Filled with admiration now, as well as desire, I am pleased to learn that he is interested in me too. One thing leads to another and soon we are sneaking up to the hay loft in the barn until the early morning hours, when I slip back to my room while pulling straw from my hair.

Eventually my father hears of my clandestine meetings with Jim, and being an unpretentious and earthy man, he is fine with it all. He's not a snob like the other rich landowners, for whom he feels disdain.

Since Jim and I love each other, my father not only supports our getting married, he gives Jim and me a large tract of land as a wedding present.

Jim and I have a long and happy life together.

My second lifetime with Jim is set in France around AD 830. Its happy beginning ends tragically for us both. This is the lifetime that hangs heavy over my relationship with Jim:

Once again, I am a young woman whose father is a successful farmer. A man of the soil who grows grapes and has a winery on his vast acreage. He is well regarded in the community and carries much clout there. Jim is a very wealthy young man; the son of a powerful landowner who resides in the same community.

When Jim and I meet we share a feeling that we already know each other. It is love at first sight for us and before long we want to get married. Our parents are delighted, as they see it as a merger of two great families. Our marriage will give both sides even more power and influence, so our wedding takes place without delay. I am fourteen and Jim is sixteen.

As young newlyweds we are so happy together, living what seems to be a perfect life and looking forward to soon becoming parents. We could never have imagined that this blissful life we have built will come crashing down in six months.

One day young Jim is riding his horse homeward at the end of a day overseeing our field hands. Suddenly he is accosted by a gang of thugs intent on robbing him. He has little money on him, but as a matter of principle—and because Jim's manly pride is challenged—he tries to fight them off.

If only he had given them what they wanted.

The highwaymen easily overpower and kill him. But they don't stop there. They are so enraged that he fought them, they mutilate his manhood and discard his remains by the side of the road.

Before long, his body is discovered—and that is when everything falls apart.

When news of this tragedy reaches me, I am devastated. I feel that my life—once so sunny—has turned to black. My dear Jim is gone and for me, life is over.

I miscarry two months later, but I don't care. It's for the best. I stop eating and simply give up. In another two months, I also am dead.

My first reaction to learning that Jim and I have other lifetimes together was thinking, "How romantic. Reunited just like the movie-couple in *Somewhere in Time*. Maybe…"

I began wondering about a new future with Jim.

Then I woke up from *that* adolescent fantasy. I realized I was holding on to the stories of our other lifetimes, which were loose ends I needed to let go of. When I consciously did that, it brought a sense of completion to my relationship with Jim.

He and I lost contact—except for one last time when I ran into him at a local charity event. He introduced me to his fiancé. Her name was Patty.

Chapter 15

Sam

One Friday afternoon in 1974, my friend Joan (a Malibu neighbor) and I drove to Beverly Hills where she would have a manicure, and then meet me afterward for drinks at the famed Luau restaurant. I left my car in the Luau parking lot and she went on her way. With an hour to kill, I stepped inside for a bite to eat.

The dining room was closed but the lounge was open. Its only patrons were four men sitting together at the bar. I sat down in a large booth and ordered some appetizers. Before my food arrived, one of the men came over and introduced himself to me. His name was Sam.

Sam, a well-dressed forty-something, was very personable and quite witty. He said he had seen me walking on the sidewalk and hoped I would come into the restaurant. As he spoke, there was something familiar about him. Then I remembered. "I met you once before in here and when you said you were married, I told you I didn't date married men." He assured me he was now divorced.

When Joan arrived, we each ordered a Mai Tai to enjoy with our appetizers. A bit later Sam and his friends asked if we wanted to join them for cocktails at the Beverly Hills Hotel's Polo Lounge. We did.

That's how my relationship with Sam began. We dated steadily for about seven years after our meeting on that day in 1974—which happened to be just a few months after my first romantic relationship with Jim had ended.

I knew my relationship with Sam would never end in marriage, something he had made clear, and eventually it ran its course.

But as things turned out, I reconnected with Sam by chance in early 1989. It seemed history was repeating itself, because Sam and I got together just a few months after my reunion with Jim had ended.

This pattern of leap-frogging relationships with these two men was hard to ignore.

During our second time around, I had a feeling that Sam and I had some unfinished business—undoubtedly related to a lifetime or two together.

In a consultation with my wise friend Ophelia, I found out about two significant lifetimes I have with Sam that are similar to the ones I have with Jim, as they have the same themes of first happiness, then tragic loss.

Yes, there is definitely a relationship-pattern in place.

Ophelia briefly described both of my lifetimes with Sam. This is what I learned about our first one together—our happily-ever-after lifetime:

> Sam and I are much revered druids, wise ones who were appointed to be healers and spiritual guides by our Celtic tribe in ancient Britain. He and I (again a woman) practice the healing arts together and become lifelong partners as a loving couple living together in harmony throughout our entire lives.

My second significant lifetime with Sam takes place in New England in the early 1800s. It has a sorrowful ending that hangs like a dark cloud over my present life:

> Sam is my beloved husband and a seaman who makes his living crewing on cargo vessels that sail the oceans to distant ports. One day he goes off to sea and just never returns. I never find out what happened to him. My heart is broken. Every day I stand at the end of the dock staring out to sea—waiting in vain for my husband to come back to me.

This pattern of having two important lifetimes—one happy, one tragic—with the same person I have a close relationship with during my current lifetime, is also repeated in the next chapter.

Eventually the *bigger picture*—the greater meaning for me—will become apparent.

Chapter 16

Matt

I first became aware of Matt in 1997 when he got the microphone at one of the metaphysical workshops I had been attending for many years. He asked the wise being-friend conducting the workshop for insights regarding a personal issue he was dealing with. I was sitting a few rows behind him, so I only saw the back of his head, but I noted how intelligent and self-aware he seemed to be when he spoke.

I attended more of those workshops through the coming months and Matt was there too. By now I knew that he was a compassionate fellow-metaphysician and *that* was most important to me. Oh yes—he was also quite handsome. I decided I'd like to meet him.

I don't remember exactly how it came about, but he and I did meet. Before long, every time we saw each other we were drawn together like two magnets—and long hugs ensued. It turned out that he lived not far from me—then dating ensued.

Matt would come to my place for a quiet evening of dinner and a movie. He always helped me prepare our food—making the salad, broiling the steaks—and it felt like we had been doing this all of our lives. It was the most natural thing. But from the beginning of our time together, I knew our romantic relationship was not going to last.

We saw each other off and on for about two years. Then in 2000, Matt moved to another state—something he had told me early-on that he was planning to do. He stopped attending the workshops held in California after he moved, and I think I only saw him once or twice after that.

During the two years that Matt and I were in a personal relationship, I was having monthly consultations alternately with two of my wise friends, Ophelia and Elanor. As always, I would have a list of personal issues about which I wanted their insights and guidance. A list that included questions about my relationship with Matt. Specifically, I wanted to know what our relationship was showing me about myself. How and why I was creating this reality with this particular person.

I learned a lot of crucial things about myself, including how I related to men in general, why I gave my power to them in exchange for potentially "being taken care of" emotionally or financially. Most importantly, I was reminded that this relationship—and *all* my other relationships with men—reflected *my* complex relationship with my own inner masculine and feminine energies—and how those energies interacted with each other (dysfunctionally, at that time).

There was much for me to recognize about myself and to let go of. Matt was the perfect man to reflect those things back to me because he had many of the same issues—which also included a fear of intimacy and commitment.

From my wise friends I also learned about two significant lifetimes Matt and I have together that were influencing our relationship, as well as impacting other areas of my life. Keeping in synch with the now-obvious pattern of my romantic relationships, one of our lifetimes is blissfully domestic, the other is tragically sad.

Naturally, Matt had a different name in each of these lifetimes, but for simplicity's sake I'll continue to refer to him as Matt. This is a brief summary of our happily married lifetime:

> Following Spain's conquest of Peru around 1532, the Roman Catholic Church sent priests there to convert the population to Catholicism. Matt and I were young converts who loved each other. We were wed in the new cathedral not far from our village. We were good and faithful Catholics who had many children during our long, happy life together.

My second significant lifetime with Matt has the familiar undertones of tragedy, abandonment, and lost love, but its story is far different from the others in this section. This lifetime takes place in the Atlantis governed as a "benevolent" dictatorship, some years before the end-times of its second civilization:

I am a female philosophy professor at the University of Atlantis. Although these are turbulent times, I am cloistered in academia and have no interest in politics, especially the goings-on of the government.

One balmy summer evening, after a full day at the university, I am walking my large dog through the empty streets of my quiet residential neighborhood. Suddenly from a darkened side street, a young man, clearly in distress, rushes up to me and pleads with me to hide him. "I am being chased by the militia and if I'm caught, they will arrest me and then kill me. Please help me."

Without hesitation, I tell him to follow me to my house— "Where you can stay for a few hours, but then you must leave." We run there together, my dog leading the way.

Once inside my house, I lock all the doors and turn off the lights. As we sit in my darkened main room, the young man, calmer now, tells me his harrowing story.

It seems he is well educated, and hails from a prominent family. Through his contacts he got a mid-level position in an important department of the central government, the body that controls all of Atlantis. During his two years in that post he has seen extensive corruption and abuse of power by government officials in all levels of the hierarchy.

Worst of all, he recently learned about the cruel ways in which the homeless, the elderly and other "non-productive" citizenry are "taken care of." They are shipped off to small outer islands, never again to be heard from. Many suspect the unfortunates are eventually eliminated.

Matt reported what he had learned to a supervisor he trusted. She is one of only two women with an executive ranking in the government. He thought she was a friend with some clout, but she betrayed him. He was identified as a traitor. A threat to the state who must be apprehended at once.

Matt learned what was in store for him by chance when he overheard a whispered conversation outside his office. He immediately left the premises and never even went home. He hid out until nightfall, then stealthily made his way out of the city. He ran as far as possible—that's when he saw me walking my dog and asked for my help.

As he told me his story I was impressed by his compassion for the unfortunates who were being so ruthlessly treated by the authorities, and by his courage in speaking out against that injustice without any regard for the retaliation he knew would follow.

I just couldn't turn him out, at least not until the authorities' urgent quest to find him subsided a bit. I told him he could stay in my guest room for two months. Then we would see if it was safe for him to leave.

As we got to know each other over those months, we discovered that we shared similar views about many things. In time our friendship became a deep love. We wanted a future together, so we made plans to move somewhere far away. Somewhere we could live a normal life as a married couple.

Before that could happen, I needed to notify the university that I was leaving and also to finalize arrangements with a co-worker who wanted to purchase my residence. I gave Matt enough money for a room and meals at a local inn, where he would stay through the week as I tied up loose ends. I managed to have dinner with him at the inn twice that week.

Our plan was to rendezvous at the fountain in the local park in seven days at exactly nine o'clock that night.

It seemed the week would never end, but at last I was standing by the fountain at the appointed time waiting for Matt to arrive. I waited all night long, but he never showed up. I was frantic. Had he been recognized and arrested? Was he injured somehow? Or did he decide to flee by himself? And worst of all, had he just been using me until he no longer needed me?

I never found out what happened to him, and never got over it.

Experiencing that sudden loss, tainted by confusion and suspicion, left a hole in my heart—and a sense of distrust—from which I never quite recovered.

Epilogue

Today is April 7, 2020. This morning I had a phone conversation with my lifelong friend Barbara in Colorado. One of the many things we talked about was this chapter about my relationship with Matt, a copy of which I had sent her. Barbara told me some painful details about a similar relationship she had had as a very young woman.

When I got off the phone, I went back to this chapter and my lifetime in Atlantis to add a few things I had left out of the last two paragraphs.

Specifically, I added these final lines: "And worst of all, had he just been using me until he no longer needed me?" At the end of the very last line I wrote: "And a sense of distrust—from which I never quite recovered."

Those last thoughts arose from the hurt and sickening suspicion of betrayal that I had suppressed until writing about them opened the door.

As I was re-reading what I had just written, I felt the pressure of a strong energy hovering above me. (This often happens when an unseen friend wants to communicate with me.)

I was wondering, "Who could this be?" I consciously opened myself to receiving and soon got a sense that this was the one I had just written about. Matt. I was surprised, to say the least. This energy was very strong and persistent, as though there was an urgency about communicating with me right now.

I was pondering various reasons that his desire to contact me was happening. We humans currently are in the midst of a worldwide epidemic caused by the so called Covid-19 virus. Maybe Matt, who lives in another state, had contracted it—or who knows what?

I Googled his name and the city in which he lives and was shocked to see the first thing that came up on the internet. It was his obituary! It had been written about his death almost exactly one year ago today. It was a lengthy piece that not only spoke of his life history but also beautifully described his wonderful qualities and, using metaphysical terms, his positive impact upon everyone who knew him.

I was stunned. There was so much to wrap my head around—including the synchronicity of having had a conversation about Matt with Barbara just this morning, revising this chapter a few minutes ago, having

Matt seeking to contact me as I wrote my painful revisions, and just now finding out that he had died a year ago. Within a few short hours, all those pieces came together as though drawn by a magnet.

After I calmed myself, I realized it was important to find out why Matt wanted to contact me.

I lay down on my bed and relaxed into a comfortable position. Then I opened my consciousness to receiving. This is what came to me:

This one, no longer physical and therefore no longer "Matt," but rather the spiritual being who is *more*, wants to reassure me (regarding our lifetime in Atlantis) that he did not decide to flee by himself, nor did he just use me until he no longer needed me. (The haunting scenarios I had imagined.)

I am made aware that the true reason he was unable to meet me as we'd planned was because someone at the inn—perhaps the owner—had recognized him as a fugitive wanted by the government and, encouraged by the reward that was offered, had reported him to the authorities. He was arrested the day before we were to leave Atlantis.

This dear one now wants me to know of the deep love they feel for me—an everlasting love that prevails throughout our many lifetimes together, including the ones I have written about here—and wants to reassure me of their love for me in *this* lifetime where I am Patty and he is Matt.

I am so grateful that this being reached out to me, as a caring and trustworthy friend, to assure me of their love. Their timely presence was a gift of healing and inner peace that ended my lingering doubts.

Chapter 17

Dave

One afternoon—in 2007, as I recall—I got a phone call from someone who had watched part of my Living Wisdom cable TV talk show that aired once a week on the local community access channel. The man who was calling had seen it earlier that day, and although he'd only caught the last five minutes of the show (which included the closing credits with my then phone number), he wanted to know more about the show and about me.

He introduced himself as Dave and we talked for quite a while. He mentioned that he was dealing with some health issues and other personal problems in his life, and he felt I would be a good person to talk to. He asked if I ever gave private consultations.

At that time, I *was* offering my services—not as a counselor, per se, but more as an intuitive life-coach—to a select few who requested my help.

I explained to Dave that I never told anyone what they should or must do. Instead, I gave them my intuitive insights and suggestion about what to look at about themselves. How and why *they* created *that* reality, by either causing it or allowing it, and some ways they could manifest a positive change.

I let him know that each hour and a half session that I had with someone included a guided meditation to allow an inner part of them—most often their inner child or adolescent— express their suppressed thoughts and feelings around a pivotal situation or event in their early life, and how those meditations always brought some degree of positive change.

Normally I would be hesitant about inviting a strange man into the sanctuary of my home, but in this case, during our long conversation I had gotten to know enough about Dave to ascertain that he was an honorable, kind-hearted person and well respected in his field. He made an appointment to see me the following evening.

Dave ended up having weekly sessions with me for about four years. During that time, I was contacted by other people who also saw my show. Oddly, each one said they'd only "caught the last five minutes" of it. Some came for private sessions and all of them, including Dave, participated in a weekly open-ended group session I conducted in my house.

All of this came about with no effort on my part—and I loved meeting with those folks and seeing the positive results that came from our working together. One woman's failing eyesight was restored after I encouraged her to see the reality of how her husband was treating her.

As things evolved with Dave, it became clear that he was resistant to my suggestions to express his feelings, such as the potent anger I could tell he had been suppressing since childhood. He was a world-class people-pleaser who seldom said "no" to a request, no matter how much he really did not want to comply with it.

I also recognized the part of him that felt obligated to sacrifice himself for others. That is called being a martyr—very unhealthy for any relationship and damaging to oneself. But Dave was deaf to my suggestions to consider these things that I saw so clearly. He had an unbending belief system by which he lived his life.

Dave was a master of a unique form of martial arts. He had been a fierce competitor when he was younger, and in later years a respected instructor. Dave adhered to the rigid discipline that was the foundation of this combative sport, the rules of which included maintaining "inner calmness" and developing "perfection of character." The exception to calmness and character seemed to be combat in the ring, where one could do great damage to their opponent using energy fueled by their suppressed rage. Dave said that was how it was for him, and the reason he won so many contests. I knew that kind of outward expression of anger was not the same as actually *feeling* it without inflicting it on someone else—and then releasing it. But he had other beliefs and I respected them.

Now retired, Dave's earlier physical injuries from years of competing (and suppressing his emotions) were crippling his body in new ways. My intuition told me he would die sooner, rather than later.

I realized that my only way to be of service to Dave was to be a good listener. Someone he could confide in, without judgment or criticism. It also seemed, from the things he said now and then, that Dave had a personal interest in me. This is one example: A month after Dave began his sessions with me, I invited a homeless woman to stay in my extra bedroom for a short time. (That's another long story.) Dave said, "When she moves out can I move in?" I knew he was kidding "on-the-square," as they say. I ignored all those kinds of comments from him.

To be honest, on some level I *was* attracted to Dave, and I sensed that he and I probably have a lifetime or two together. Eventually I asked my wise friend Elanor about that possibility. By the time I did so, I had gained a lot more wisdom about the importance of being an objective observer of my reality and the others in it. Meaning, to be less caught up in the details of the stories and instead to see the situation as feedback from which to learn about myself.

In my taped conversation with Elanor, this is how I described my situation with Dave (keeping in mind that at *that* time I was still interested in someday having a romantic relationship with a partner):

"My relationship with Dave is like a science project. An opportunity to experiment in a relationship right under my roof. But he is not the one for me. He is cut off from his feelings. He seems superficial (today I would say *not present*). He is a people-pleaser 'nice guy.' Neither true to himself, nor truthful with himself."

(Of course, I would never have said those things to Dave.)

This was Elanor's response:

"This relationship was valuable. See it as a pie. A quarter piece was: 'I learned that I am still attractive to men—very important to me.' A quarter piece was: 'He showed me parts of my disowned self. I am ultra-honest, ultra-responsible, ultra-aware of emotions, but I have an opposite, disowned self (the other half of the pie) which Dave is showing me. I need to own *that* part of me and integrate it."

Then I asked if Dave and I have some lifetimes together. This is the one Elanor briefly described that influences our current relationship:
"In one lifetime together, he owns a ski resort. You are a girl, much younger than he is, who works there. As time passes, he becomes very attracted to you, and you feel the same about him. He is an honorable man and although you love each other, you cannot be together in any way because he is married to a woman his same age. Eventually his wife dies, and you are finally free to be together. You get married and live very happily until his death."

That lifetime explained several things about my situation with Dave. I believe that when he saw me briefly on TV, he wasn't drawn in by what I was saying, but rather by the familiarity of my energies. That is why we were never on the same wavelength in our communication. His rigid belief system was opposite from my own, based in the metaphysical concept of continual growth and change where open mindedness, and flexibility are essential.

Although Dave bought me small presents and made little remarks that *implied* he would like to have a personal relationship with me, he never did or said more. He was a married man for the first two years of our weekly sessions. Then he told me he was going to divorce his wife because of something she did. I encouraged him to seek marriage counseling first. But he was adamant, and he did get a divorce.

For the next two years I remained someone he could talk to, could confide in like a friend, but there was no possibility of any other kind of relationship. That would have been unethical for me—and I was not interested in him in that way.

Around the four years mark, something came up in Dave's life that required him to be out of town for six months. I also was making some changes in my life which included changing my phone number. I never gave Dave my new unlisted number and our relationship ended in a natural way.

When I began writing this chapter, I decided to Google Dave's full name to bring me up to date on his life. I learned that he had died nine years before at a relatively young age, just as I felt he might.

Chapter 18

At Last

I finally have the answer to a question I had asked myself on that certain summer's day in 1985, the one I mention in the first chapter of this book, that asks "Why did I—so self-sufficient and independent—always need to have a man in my life?"

It has taken thirty-five-plus years of gaining more and more self-awareness and wisdom—as well as understanding the relationships I've had with a variety of men—for me to reach this answer: The loving, intimate and everlasting relationship I was seeking all along was the relationship I needed to have with myself—and with my own inner masculine energies.

It is easy to see now, in retrospect, that many long standing issues and feelings that I chose to deal with during this lifetime—my sense of powerlessness, abandonment and betrayal, my fears, blame, and anger—stemmed from underlying beliefs and attitudes I've held toward men and all that is masculine. That includes a bias against my own inner masculine, so out of balance with my feminine self.

The impact of harboring such issues and emotions is demonstrated in the lifetime stories I have related in this section. What better way to reveal those impedances to happiness and success than to bring them out of the shadows and into the light by engaging in a variety of relationships and lifetimes with different men?

Every relationship has been an opportunity to learn more about who I am and who I am becoming as a spiritual human being—and to gain a deeper understanding and compassion for the complexities of being human—the *human condition.*

I have found that from having compassion and understanding arises *unconditional* love for myself and for *all that is*—a divine creation. The divine I know as God/Goddess—inseparable masculine and feminine energies continually balancing and harmonizing with each other, as they powerfully create and recreate new realities from unconditional love.

Older and wiser now, I know there is no need to search "out there" for love. I can simply open myself to expressing it and receiving it.

Luminous Lifetimes of Expanded Wisdom

Chapter 19

Patriot

c. 1770s
New England

For a long time, I have readily accepted that many of my lifetimes are difficult and painful ones clinging to the lower rungs of existence, and I have gotten to know lots of them. What I learned from my wise friend Elanor in an early 2016 consultation gave me quite a different perspective of the entire panorama of my lifetimes and why I am living this one.

As Elanor put it, "You have a tendency to see your lifetimes as 'I've had a bunch of lifetimes because I screwed them up and I have to come and fix them.' And that is so not true.

'I have a lot of lifetimes because I wanted to experience every possible variation of what it means to be a human being. The entire range from incredibly spiritual and beautiful to twisted and horrible, because I need all of that. I am going to use all those diverse threads because what they have in common is that they will help to create a new paradigm. With those threads I am going to weave a new paradigm. A new concept for humanity itself.'

You're lucky you have lots of help to do that part."

Elanor continued: "The important thing here is to shift your perspective so that you truly *get* that you are gathering up those threads and every single one is important. Every single one is precious and valuable and beautiful."

This chapter is about one of those important and beautiful lifetimes.

I've always felt that I have a lifetime in which I participate in some way in the origin of the United States, the Declaration of Independence, and the Bill of Rights. That I am somehow involved in establishing our independence from England and the formation of our government. Early on when those thoughts came to me, I cautioned myself against self-delusion. "No Patty, you were not John Hancock or Thomas Jefferson."

In early 2016, I learned of a lifetime that takes place when the founding fathers are endeavoring to create a sovereign nation, following the colonies' hard-won independence from England.

In my first meditation that guided me to that lifetime, I experience actually *being* that one. The setting is New England. This was my experience:

I sense myself as a man wearing mid-length breeches tied just below my knees, long white stockings, and shoes adorned with large buckles. I wear a white powdered wig, as is the fashion. I seem to be an elderly man whose sage counsel is sought and respected. (Not knowing his name, I shall refer to him as Patriot.)

I really feel myself present. Really feel I am here at this gathering of men in a schoolhouse. It is a congress of sorts, not the formal kind, to discuss what the future of our country should be and how we will get there as we seek to create a separate government to end our dependence upon and control by England.

Consciously opening myself to experiencing Patriot's energies, I feel a harmonious balancing of them within me. A sense of being at one with our truer self. Being grounded in this reality as our truer self.

I am in a conversation with one who will be a key player in the formation of the United States (perhaps it is John Adams) and I suggest, in a subtle way, that the goal of the new government and the formation documents, the Declaration of Independence and the Constitution, should be inclusivity of all citizens—to give equal rights to all citizens under the Constitution.

I want us to create new forms. To reshape the judicial system with laws that will be more favorable to the common person. To be more equitable. To not be an elitist government in the hands of a few, as is being contemplated at this time. That kind of domination and control is what we are seeking independence from.

Coming out of the meditation I feel deep gratitude for this connection, and my love for America.

A few weeks later I did a second meditation to experience being my Patriot lifetime:

I find myself again in a room with other men who are formulating the foundation of the country. I am having a conversation with Benjamin Franklin. Franklin speaks to me about how much he likes the finer things in life and how he admires the upper-class lifestyle, especially that of the French aristocracy with their lavish surroundings and their finery. He loves their whole way of living.

I listen to him patiently, and then I remind him that he, himself, came from very humble origins. I tactfully say that something important to keep in mind is that in our country, our new country that is going to be formed, most of the population has the same humble origins and lives in the same humble surroundings as he once had. They are people of the land.

I suggest strongly that our new country be founded upon the principle of equal opportunity for all. Equal opportunity to aspire to more and to achieve more. And that the Constitution be written in a way to provide equal opportunities for those common folks. To not be exclusive of them. To be written for the people and by the people.

I am filled with understanding and compassion for Ben Franklin. I do not judge or criticize him for admiring and seeking the finer things for his life. I look into his eyes and feel our connection based upon our mutual feelings of compassion for others. I sense him being influenced by my words and my presence.

Now I experience myself in this lifetime as a light in this room. As a light of inspiration having impact on those gathered here.

My third meditative experience begins as a visitor to Patriot's home:

I am in front of a white clapboard two-storied house with a porch-veranda stretching across the front of the house. I knock on the door and that one—in male form—invites me into his parlor. He has been waiting for me and a tea service is on a small table. We talk for a while (but I don't recall what was said).

While still in this meditation, the term "luminous hope" comes to me and I segue into a process called "Divine Co-Creation," which I learned from my wise friend Elanor.

Working my way through each of its seven steps, from Apprehension to Luminous Hope, opens me to the vibrational frequencies of luminous hope, feeling their resonance within me, as a part of me. I experience how it would be possible to manifest a whole new type of human being and a whole new paradigm. In that resonance I sense the light of the Goddess within me.

The emotions I feel in the Patriot lifetime–compassion and luminous hope–also fill me now. I see the Statue of Liberty as the Goddess holding high her lamp of freedom that illuminates the way toward a new world in a new paradigm.

When I told my wise friend Elanor about my experiences in my Patriot lifetime, this is what they said: "So you gathered the threads of compassion and hope and wove them together, and with authority and wisdom found the dignity and character, and created a bridge from that lifetime to this lifetime—and to many others."

Experiencing this Patriot lifetime helped me let in, at a deeper level, what several wise friends have told me about my having an inner light and a healing energy that touches those around me. I felt the truth of it.

Every single lifetime that anyone has is valuable. The lifetimes that follow show how beautiful and magical and fun they can be.

Chapter 20

Aramai—
Crystal Temple Priest
Atlantis, 3rd Civilization

One Sunday afternoon—in 2012, as I recall—I attended a workshop conducted by Dr. Peebles and Torah, two wise channeled beings I knew well. During the workshop they each shared higher truths about that day's topic related to personal and spiritual growth. Then they took our small group on a guided meditation, after which we were invited to make comments and ask questions.

When it was my turn, I mentioned that for many years I had been exploring my own spiritual journey by connecting with many of my other lifetimes—most of them with painful realities and challenges—getting to know and understand them and then integrating them. Now I felt ready to move beyond my limited-self lifetimes and to begin experiencing the more enlightened ones.

I asked if they could tell me about any of my lifetimes that are grounded, as spiritual adults, in the knowledge that they create every second of their reality. Perhaps there is one who can help me at this time be in that same place of dominion as a spiritual human being *consciously* creating a positive reality—creating my heart's desire.

I recorded their responses on my trusty—but low-tech—tape recorder. This is what Torah had to say:

"You *have* had, well, up to three lifetimes like that. We sense one that, paradoxically—we say paradoxically because it was in a culture that was fraught with some conflict, and that's in Atlantis—we *do* sense you in that (lifetime). It was involved with crystals, very much so. A crystal temple. You may have a sense of it now and then, regarding crystals, in the present lifetime: 'Been there done that. Don't know if I need to do that as intensely now.' You may have had that feeling more than once. And that's because—whoa—you were *extremely* dedicated to them.

So, you were a woman in that life, and you taught. And it's very interesting because you were very aware that the students in your classes were a reflection of you in many ways, and you used *that* as a way to be looking at the many aspects of yourself that you needed to integrate and to learn about.

But you reached a certain point in your life with a certain maturity—though age is irrelevant—in the aging that it would take, and in your knowingness as a creator of reality, and in the magic that you did with the crystals, of backing up a little bit from interaction with all those students because you had watched them long enough, to the degree that suddenly it was as though *that* was no longer relevant to you.

So, then you enjoyed observing how *they* created *their* reality. Very interesting in that way.

It was a lifetime of learning, learning, learning and teaching, teaching, teaching and then observing, observing, observing.

So that's one we can tell you about. She stayed very conscious of creating her reality, but through these rather different attitudes—one as student, one as teacher, one as observer. The long white robes, all the eclectic white robes, were there."

I asked if Torah wanted to tell me her name. "You can find it on your own. It begins with A."

Dr. Peebles suggested that I place myself in a grid or a matrix of crystals, like a pyramid, bringing forth a concentration of energies. Adding, "If you relax into it, there is so much that will bubble up from your unconscious that you will find a form of self-empowerment in the choices you make, in this (physical) time and space, where you now second-guess yourself."

Shortly after the workshop, I took my first meditative journey to that lifetime and I learned that her name was Aramai.

As I continue writing this chapter about Aramai it is mid-April 2020, a time of great turbulence in the world. I endeavor to not get caught up in the rampant anger, fear and confusion that prevails at this time, especially in America. As a metaphysician, I choose to learn from what is taking place as a compassionate observer. But that is a choice I must make over and over throughout each day.

Getting to know and understand this more enlightened lifetime known as Aramai is absolutely in synch with where I am right now. For so many years I have focused on obtaining self-knowledge through seeing others as reflections and projections of aspects—usually the more limited ones—of multi-faceted me. Then I've processed their issues and integrated those aspects into the greater being we are.

Much of that self-discovery has involved exploring my other lifetimes— and some of those lifetimes are chapters in this book. But now I am ready to step back and become the observer—just as Aramai does—filled with compassion and understanding for others, but emotionally detached from their personal dramas, trials, and tribulations—*their* lifetime stories.

I'm certain that getting to know and understand Aramai, and then integrating her (our) more expansive energies will help me be that more enlightened version of my truer self.

This is my experience, quite unlike any other, in the meditation I just did:
In my familiar safe place, I invite my soul to join me. I sense them as an elongated sphere of white light before me. I tell them I wish to experience the lifetime known as Aramai, to get to know that one and to understand them. I call upon my soul to transport me to that lifetime. Within the light of my soul, I surrender to powerlessness and I sense myself being lifted into the ethers. As I relax into their light, I sense myself drifting this way and that through time and space until I begin a gentle descent.

Feeling solid ground under my feet I now step out of the light and find myself in a vast room. It is a temple and before me is a female wearing long robes, beautiful robes with designs on them I don't recognize. I know this is Aramai and I introduce myself as another aspect of the greater being we are who has come to get to know her and to understand what she does. Aramai understands this and she welcomes me. "We've been waiting for you."

She leads me to an altar of sorts—a waist-high solid marble rectangle—centered before a huge wall with a large array of different kinds of crystals displayed in niches created to hold each of them. The display's overall design is a tall pyramid, with its wide base located behind the marble altar.

Aramai invites me to lie upon the marble altar which is thickly padded with a tufted velvet-like fabric of a deep amethyst color. I see that she holds in each hand a small double ended cylinder of clear crystal about four inches long. As I lie quietly on the padded table with my eyes closed, she puts her right hand and the crystal at the top of my head where my seventh chakra is and moves her left hand over each of my lower chakras. I hear a constant tone—an Ohm sound—in this enormous room, but I can't tell if Aramai is the source.

She continues to deftly move both hand-held crystals up and down in a deliberate pattern, repeatedly touching each chakra in turn. This deep-healing session concludes with what feels like a bolt of white light rushing through me and, at the same time, out of my head and my feet. Aramai offers her hand to help me step down.

Now she leads me to the opposite end of this long room to stand before a gigantic generator crystal. It is so tall it extends through the high ceiling, into the roof of the building and beyond—its tapering faceted tip piercing the sky. This huge crystal rests upon a round, a kind of turntable, decorated with rune-like characters.

I learn that only the High Priests, one of whom is Aramai, have the authority—and the ability—to move the turntable, for this crystal and the others like it collectively provide all of the electro-magnetic energy that runs Atlantis.

I also learn that my visit coincides with the dangerous times of the great culture-clash near the end of the third civilization of Atlantis when certain metaphysical zealots, some of whom are High Priests, are determined to destroy the corrupt and brutal government of Atlantis. They plan to do this by repositioning this crystal, and the four other giant crystals located on outlier islands surrounding the great land mass that is central Atlantis. By concentrating the EM energies on the seat of governmental rule, they believe they can destroy just that target.

Aramai's is a strong voice of sanity and reason attempting to dissuade the other Priests from taking that drastic action. Gifted with prescience, she knows the result will be total annihilation. The crystals will implode, and the land of Atlantis will disappear forever.

Her rational words are ignored.

In a quiet moment, she reminds herself that the others are simply reflections of the more limited aspects of her truer self—the greater spiritual being *they* are together. With an open heart, Aramai accepts and respects the others just as they are. With compassion and open arms, she integrates them into the oneness—their united states of being.

The others will create *their* realities in the holographic illusion of the physical world—and Aramai will create the reality she prefers.

I understand why my lifetime as Aramai was important to visit just when I did, and why they said, "We've been waiting for you."

I also understand why today I was compelled to revise these last paragraphs. The chaotic times in her Atlantis are reflections of the turbulence and unsolvable problems happening now in the year 2020.

Reviewing Aramai's enlightened response to her situation reminded me and inspired me to respond to my world—where our crises are escalating—in this way:

In this moment, with commitment and determination, I fully accept myself just as I am—the lesser and the more—and I take responsibility for creating *my* reality, this time letting it be brand new—even beyond what I can envision. I choose to be present and *alive*—filled with hope and joy and expectation.

I own my power to manifest reality—and I see a light at the end of the tunnel.

Chapter 21

A Visionary in Atlantis
A Modern Utopia; Atlantean Healing Center

I t seems that most people believe that Atlantis is simply a mythical place that never existed. Of those who do believe in its existence, including many authors of books on the subject, the consensus view is that Atlantis was an ancient land located somewhere in the Atlantic Ocean until it was destroyed by a cataclysmic event. Some believers also hold that there were three civilizations of Atlantis, each of which was destroyed.

What I believe is that *all* of those versions of the story of Atlantis are true—a paradox based upon the concept that diverse realities exist in different dimensions of the unconscious realm. I also believe that there are always higher truths—truths that offer more personal freedom and require more personal responsibility—that make possible alternate realities of unlimited beauty and prosperity.

A Modern Utopia:
This chapter is about adventures I had in an Atlantis most have never heard of, but one that is known to me thanks to higher truths I learned from several wise friends and the soul-guided meditations that took me there.

In December 2016, my curiosity inspired me to explore a version of Atlantis that not only was never destroyed, but one that has a vibrant, prosperous, and peaceful society. A modern utopia. What I experienced in my first soul-guided meditation was unexpected and amazing. It also revealed details that answered many questions.

This is what I learned about present-day Atlantis:

I find myself in the City of Atlantis, the largest metropolis on the continent of Atlantis. This is a bustling city, as most large ones are, but Atlantis differs in every other way.

I sense the peace and harmony that prevails here. People here have compassion for one another and they live in peaceful cooperation, accepting and respecting each other without criticism or judgment. There is a sense of balance and harmony throughout this society. All have equal value, not because it has been legislated so, but because everyone knows in the core of their being it is true.

I see tall buildings here in the heart of this beautiful city. Each structure has many windows and seems to be made of solid materials, much like concrete and marble. The buildings are in lighter colors to reflect the heat of the day.

Everyone here wears the light colored, loose fitting garments most suitable for a warm climate, for this continent of Atlantis lies near the same latitude as our Caribbean—in the holographic reality that is planet Earth.

The air and coastal waters of Atlantis are warmed by the strong current that flows northward along its eastern coastline, until the warm stream curves eastward beyond land into the vast ocean we call Atlantic. (Please see Note below.)

There are wide thoroughfares in this thriving city designed for vehicles powered by electromagnetic energy. Each vehicle has a crystal sphere which receives EM energy from the giant crystals that generate power for all of Atlantis. A vehicle's sphere is kept in a compartment made to contain it depending on its size. Larger vehicles have larger crystals.

Every vehicle is aerodynamically styled and skims, like a hovercraft, over the surface of the street.

The whole of Atlantis is powered by giant generator crystals— each about a hundred feet tall—which are strategically placed in a power grid surrounding the city at its farthest boundaries on outlier islands in the offshore waters.

Those crystals, like all crystals, absorb energy and release energy. (In the reality where Atlantis is annihilated, its destruction comes about when the giant generator crystals implode, creating a "black hole" into which all matter is drawn.)

Each of the Atlantean crystals is calibrated specifically to serve its particular purpose and location by technicians with the unique skills and sensitivity to do so, under the direction of the High Priests in charge.

Perfection is a state of being not sought nor expected here. There are various healing centers that re-tune and re-align energies in different ways using crystals, sounds, and colors. These centers are always available for anyone who requests such assistance. Most are for humans, but others offer aid to animals. Intuitive healers, called priests (a non-religious title), provide help to anyone seeking their services.

As I stand in this place, I sense myself to be one who is present in this utopian civilization to hold the space for it in the physical world, and to fill this space with light as a visionary resonating with luminous hope. This Atlantis is a reflection and an expression of the being I am, just as are all the realities in all my lifetimes.

There are others here who also resonate in ways that co-create this space of unconditional love and happiness and peace. I know them to be friends from Sirius who have chosen to be present in this time and space of Atlantis. Our common purpose is to imprint a paradigm—one never before manifested—for a new kind of human being and a new civilization, without the need for the destruction, the tearing down, of the old.

(Note: We know the warm current as the Gulf Stream that flows northeast from the Gulf of Mexico. In the alternate "total destruction of Atlantis" reality that occurred in about 10,800 BC, its entire landmass disappeared, which allowed the warm Gulf Stream to flow freely upward along the coastline of what is now North America, continuing past the Newfoundland coast before flowing into the North Atlantic Sea. The drastic climate change produced by the redirection of that warm current effectively ended the Ice Age and brought about either the extinction of plants and animals inhabiting northern regions, including the woolly mammoth, or it expedited their evolution—thus allowing their survival.)

Atlantean Healing Center:
Six years before my 2016 meditation to observe life in Atlantis, I did the following meditation for a quite different reason. I wanted to restore a sense of peace within myself, after an upsetting event had just occurred in my life.

As my meditation began, I called upon my soul to transport me to a place where I would be filled with energies of peace, composure, and confidence. Unexpectedly, that place was an Atlantean healing center, something I had never heard of. This is some of what I experienced:

I am transported through the ethers until I sense myself gently descending to solid ground. I find myself in Atlantis standing before a gigantic cathedral, called a High Temple, in which crystals are kept.

I enter the temple and walk into a vast room with a tall generator crystal at the far end. I know my soul is here with me. I allow myself to be impacted by the powerful healing energies that emanate from this crystal. I can sense the changes in my atomic makeup. I begin to feel peacefulness, composure and confidence resonating within me—filling me. I just let it be what it is, until I sense this healing is concluded.

After the mediation, I felt the changes within me. At peace once again.

In December 2016 I was coping with another difficult situation in my current life, one that stirred up latent feelings of guilt, shame, and sorrow buried within me. I knew it was time to visit the Atlantean healing center in another meditation. My recollection of this healing experience is richer and more detailed than my earlier one:

Once again, my soul transports me to Atlantis and I find myself standing before the entrance to a magnificent building with tall doors, and columns supporting its front portico. I know this is a healing center that provides services to all who request them.

I climb the steps and turn the metal handle on one of the doors. Though it appears to be heavy, the door easily swings open.

I enter a large chamber, softly lit. It is comforting just to be here. A man in simple white robes comes forward to greet me. I feel welcome and safe, not just from his greeting but by his gentle presence. He has long white hair and a bald pate. His kind eyes emanate warmth.

He asks me to come sit with him and tell him what brings me here. I speak about a young acquaintance I had invited to live with me. My intention was to provide support and guidance that might enable her to become a self-sufficient person. Something she wanted so much. But she lost her way using drugs. Consuming more and more to escape from her life.

Finally, I had to ask her to leave and now I feel so guilty about that. I am afraid she will not make it and it will be my fault for not doing enough or being enough to help her change. I am ashamed that I made mistakes. That I wasn't good enough. I fear what may happen to her and I have such sadness about her painful life.

As I say these things, I feel deep sorrow and weep softly trying to get the words out.

This wise healer tells me, "There is no one to blame. She is making her choices. You have no power to change them or her."

He assures me that I did enough. Did the right things to help her. "It was her choice to withdraw from you."

(As I write about these thoughts and feelings now in 2020, I realize I still have suppressed guilt and sorrow about "not doing enough" for my mentally ill daughter, who has lived a difficult and painful life. The healer's words are meant for me now, just as they were when I did this meditation years ago.)

This wise one guides me to a bed on a platform in the center of the room. I lie on my back and he covers me with a thin blanket. The bed is comfortable and the temperature in this chamber is just right for me. Warm enough. He stands next to me and the lights dim to a softer glow. I close my eyes and a light cloth is placed over them.

I hear the sounds of gongs being tapped at each end of the chamber, then the light tinkling of bells. I somehow know that the healer is using his hands to shift and lift energies—like pulling taffy—from each of my seven chakra centers, beginning with the first one in front of my pelvic area. In turn, the corresponding color of each chakra fills the room and I sense myself being bathed in it.

At the end of my healing treatment, this wise one tells me, "Let *her* go free and set yourself free."

Thanks to this meditation, I felt great relief and freedom afterwards—and also now as I write about it.

Chapter 22

In the Temple of My Soul
Meeting an Unknown Presence

Some years ago, I did a meditation to visit the temple of my soul for the first time. The temple appeared to me as a round, open air, Grecian-style gazebo made of white marble. It had seven ionic columns lifting its domed roof and seven steps encircling its foundation. The temple's elevated floor was polished green malachite with three inlaid hoops of gold evenly spaced within its circumference. Between the rings were rune-like designs outlined in gold and embedded in the floor. I have visited this temple many times in meditation. It is always the same.

As I was progressing with this book, by mid-2016 I knew it was time for me to get to know and write about more of my lifetimes that exist at expanded levels of consciousness. Wiser, more enlightened lifetimes that are aspects of my greater and still unknown presence, once described by my wise friend Elanor as ninety percent of my whole being. Integrating our energies would complete my process.

My intuition told me that the temple of my soul would be the appropriate place for these introductions to take place.

Here are my experiences with some of the lifetimes I met in a series of meditations:

Kalen:

> Standing with my soul in the center of the temple floor, I invite lifetimes that are unknown aspects of my truer self to come

forward. One being arises from the outer steps and joins me in the temple. At first, I sense it is a male wearing a simple white caftan-type gown. He has white hair, balding on top. He says he has been waiting for me to call. After we greet each other I ask his name. "Kalen," he replies. I tell him I would like to know about him—this lifetime of mine. I want to experience his reality. With intention, I become one with him, merging my energies with his.

I find myself at a level of consciousness with others here, similarly dressed in simple white robes. I feel a harmonious balancing of energies resonating within me and with the others present.

I realize there are no children here and that this dimension of reality is manifested by mature spiritual beings. Also, it appears that all who are present have no gender. The robes worn emphasize the lack of gender definition.

I understand now that my initial impression of Kalen was simply what I could let in at that moment. How I automatically defined him as a male who looked a certain way using my "common senses," which do not apply here.

In this dimension of consciousness, being in body-form or being light-energy is simply a choice. Both of those states are possible here.

I open myself to incorporating the energies in this environment—filling myself with them—being them. I understand that I am experiencing a more enlightened state of beingness, one that I can access at any time—in or out of meditation.

A Being of Light:

As I stand in the center of the temple of my soul, a majestic being of light stands on the top step at floor level but does not enter the temple.

They hold in their outstretched arms a newborn infant emanating a brilliant white light. I understand that this infant symbolizes the birth—the initiation—of my relationship with the seven faces of my soul, each of which comes forward at a certain time throughout each lifetime as a step in the maturing process.

I sense that as *I* change and grow and become *more* in my current lifetime, the seven faces of my soul and their relevant stages of development that are present in *all* of my lifetimes will also evolve.

Each stage, from infancy to old age, will expand to higher vibrational frequencies as we transition together toward greater enlightenment, for we are all traveling our soul's journey Home.

(I know the faces [phases] of the soul, and when each one comes forward, to be: The Name, at birth; The Power, around eighteen months; Eternal Youth, in adolescence; The Wounding, sometime during youth; The Shadow, young adult through middle age; The Double, around fifty; and The Remains, towards the end of one's physical incarnation.)

A Future Lifetime in a New Paradigm:

Standing in the temple, I extend an unspoken invitation for a future lifetime to join me—as my wise friend Elanor had recently suggested. A being, in female form, comes forward whose name I intuit is Alyssa.

In silent communication I express my wish to experience her reality by being her. With that, I feel my energies being drawn into hers.

It seems we exist in another paradigm in a different time and space far beyond the old "separate-and unequal" paradigm manifested by chauvinism.

This is a paradise existing as it was before the concept of separateness changed everything.

I sense that the Eden mentioned in the Bible is like a fairy tale version of this reality—but with a male chauvinistic twist.

My Alyssa lifetime is happening now in a different space-time dimension that resonates with the vibrational frequencies of balance and harmony, peaceful co-operation, compassion and understanding. A new paradigm of beauty, peace, and infinite possibilities.

A Future Lifetime in Multi-Verses:

Once again in the temple, I call forth another future lifetime. Now feeling their presence with my uncommon senses, I open to integrating their energies with mine—and I begin experiencing their reality.

Expanding and expanding my consciousness more and more I am experiencing so many wondrous things. Universes where beautiful realities change in the moment—some changing in cooperation with other beings of light also present. New universes and worlds are manifested simply by imagining them.

At one point I sense the opportunity of leaving my Patty Paul lifetime—which now seems like another lifetime—and inhabiting (focusing my attention on) this expanded level of consciousness. The transition would be effortless for my light body.

I learned from this experience how easily realities can be changed with grace and elegance simply by desire and choice. A choice that might include transforming from a physical to a non-physical state of being. A transformation that is known as consciously dying.

A Light-Hearted Being:

Upon my invitation, one joins me in the temple and embraces me as though *they* are welcoming *me*. They say they have been waiting for me to come to them in this way. They have a light-hearted spirit, filled with happiness and enthusiasm.

As I begin my process of integrating them, I sense it is actually my energies being integrated into theirs. This is their reality and I am their other lifetime!

They tell me this is a different universe. One filled with lightness and joy and fun. They encourage me to "lighten up." To not take everything so seriously. "All the stories mean nothing."

I do feel myself lighter and freer, sensing that I can have this same freedom and lightness of being in my Patty Paul reality. An inner shift occurs—a new attitude that frees me from my lesser-self's compulsion to be absorbed in other people's stories, as well as my own.

I let in at a deeper level that everyone is on their own soul's journey and I have no idea what theirs might be.

What a relief!

After this meditation I went to my back patio to water some plants. A small rock with silver particles glittering in the sunlight caught my eye. I keep it as a reminder of this sense of freedom and lightness of being.

Rock with silver
particles

Five Wise Ones:

In a meditation I did in 2016 on July 23rd—a date that marks the annual opening of the Sirius vortex, the etheric portal into our universe—upon my invitation a group of five beings comes forth.

They inform me that I am also one of their group. We are known as wise ones who perform a service of counseling those who seek us out for help and guidance with personal issues and to assist in settling differences between people in our community.

I learn that we encourage and guide people to express their feelings as part of the healing process.

It seems that these beings are from an interim reality between the old paradigm and a new paradigm. It is a transitional world—a prelude to, or initial phase of a more utopian society moving toward a totally new and unimagined paradigm.

Meeting these aspects of my unknown presence—these enlightened lifetimes I am living right now in alternate realties—has given me a deeper understanding of who I truly am and my life's purpose.

For so long I believed that I must "fix" all the lesser parts of myself before I was good enough. Spiritual enough.

Now I know that I already am.

Chapter 23

A Visionary in Paradise

One summer's day in 2017 I decided to embark upon a meditative journey to experience a state of being far beyond our physical plane's limitations of time and space. Far beyond our current paradigm with its chauvinist mind-set, based upon separation, domination and control, that now is creating an "It's either them or me, dog-eat-dog, survival-of-the-fittest" kind of world.

I wanted to experience a brand-new paradigm manifested from unconditional love, acceptance, and mutual respect.

I was aware that such utopian realities exist within different dimensions of the multi-leveled unconscious realm, and that they are all happening now. Since I create my own reality, I knew I could experience a new paradigm in a self-guided meditation. "What would it feel like to be there?" I wondered, assuming I would land in one particular lifetime.

What I found was so much more.

First, I stated my intention for this meditation, then I called upon my unseen friends and my unknown presence (aspects of my wiser self) to help and guide me on this adventure into the unknown.

As usual, I began my meditation by counting down from seven to one, taking my consciousness deeper and deeper—through my subconscious as the numbers got smaller—then deeper still into the unconscious realm. At number one, I sensed myself in my familiar safe place—sensing the colors, aromas, sounds and touch that make my safe place real.

After inviting my higher self and soul to blend their energies with mine, I asked to be transported to a place beyond chauvinism where an aspect of me—a more enlightened part of the truer me—is spontaneously creating my heart's desire. And then—

Suddenly I found myself in a series of beautiful settings–flowering gardens, sunlit green meadows, cascading waterfalls–scenes that segued easily from one to another. I knew these wonderful realities were spontaneous expressions of my own inner beauty and self-love. In one enchanting space the word "paradise" came to me.

I had a desire to experience universal peace and harmony and immediately found myself standing among animals of all varieties–including lions, lambs and birds–all existing in peaceful harmony far beyond the old paradigm's "kill or be killed" laws of nature." Far beyond the ecological food-chain requirements of the physical world. I was reminded of a famous painting that depicted such animals living together in harmony.

My conscious-self wondered if this reality could ever exist in the physical world. "Eden" popped into my head, which opened me to thoughts about how much of the Bible is written as allegory and metaphor for realities I was now experiencing.

Just then another beautiful scene spontaneously manifested in which I found myself at a gathering of other beings in human form. We were all friends–a community–and many others soon joined us. I sensed that some here were friends of mine from other lifetimes in Sirius, Lemuria, and Atlantis–and from my current Patty Paul lifetime.

Unconditional love and compassion, acceptance and respect, forgiveness and gratitude were some of the emotions we shared, creating a rapport between us. I had a true sense of belonging and harmony.

Not only were my experiences in this meditation far beyond my expectation, I found that fulfilling my heart's desire to be in a whole new paradigm exposed me to new vistas, new horizons, and unlimited possibilities.

Author's Meditation and Blending Techniques

Throughout this book, I frequently mention doing self-guided meditations (using self-hypnosis) as my way of connecting with my other lifetimes. Sometimes I also speak of blending my energies with another being's as a form of communication.

Rather than describing each process every time it is mentioned, I have detailed these steps that I follow for meditations and blendings:

Meditation technique:
In a comfortable position, either sitting up or lying down, I completely relax my body, slowly inhaling and exhaling deeply three or four times, then breathing normally.

I set my intention for the meditation, which might be my desire to connect with a lifetime of mine (or with another facet of myself) that relates to an issue, relationship, or event in my current life. Or perhaps I want to experience a lifetime in a specific reality. Then I call upon my unseen friends and my unknown presence to help and guide me through the meditation.

Beginning with the number seven, I start slowly counting myself down, going deeper and deeper, through my subconscious, deeper still into my unconscious, down, down, down. At the number one I sense myself in my safe place—a private place in nature of my own design, where nature's elements—water, earth, air, and fire—are present.

Repeating the number one, I open my mental eyes and take in my surroundings with my common senses—opening to the colors, aromas, sounds, and touch that make my safe place real.

My personal safe place is a beautiful blue lagoon in a special location, with a white sandy shoreline that leads on my left to a verdant tropical forest; and on my right rounds a large boulder, then disappears beyond the next bend. The sky is blue and the golden mid-day sun is warm. The ocean air has a saltiness mixed with the fragrance of tropical flowers.

I invite my soul to join me, and soon sense their presence before me, either in human form or as a sphere of light. I express my intention for this meditation and ask them to transport me to the appropriate location. They embrace me, and with closed eyes, I rest my head on their shoulder, surrendering myself to powerlessness.

I sense myself being lifted into the ethers, gently wafting this way and that through time and space and beyond, until I feel myself descending. When my feet touch solid ground, I open my mental eyes.

I take in my surroundings, once again using my common senses. What am I standing on? Is it day or night? Is this a village? A garden? A clearing in a forest? Opening myself to receiving—allowing whatever is there to come to me. Participating, not anticipating.

What I experience in my meditations is described in each chapter.

Blending technique:
Feeling calm and relaxed, I open myself to receiving. Using my uncommon senses, I say to myself, "I sense the presence of (the one I am willing to blend with—known or unknown to me). I sense their substance. I sense their light and warmth. I sense their movement. And I sense their voice (their impact). As I am sensing their energies, I draw them into my own energies—merging them, integrating them—blending with them in that way. Then I open to expanded levels of consciousness to intuitively communicate with this entity.

This is a form of channeling that becomes more effective with practice.

The choice to do a blending is to be made consciously. When first trying this blending process, I suggest that one's higher self be called upon to be the "gatekeeper," to prevent random entities from entering one's personal space.

We *do* create our own reality. All of it. All the time. Taking responsibility for our own safety and security is empowering. Not doing so opens the door to becoming a victim.

Lemuria and Atlantis

Many of the lifetimes in this book take place in the ancient lands of Lemuria and the three civilizations of Atlantis. To provide a more comprehensive context for those lifetimes, I have included the following information about Lemuria and Atlantis, which is my interpretation of what I learned from Lazaris and other wise friends:

Lemuria:
The ancient continent of Lemuria was located in the vast ocean we call Pacific. Its landmass was cloaked in a fine mist that made luminescent the colors of flowers and greenery and light. Lemuria was created as an expression and reflection of the Goddess's divine energies in the physical world of planet Earth. Each of Lemuria's civilizations became highly advanced and spiritually evolved and when their purpose on Earth was fulfilled, Lemuria disappeared into the ethers.

Lemuria's northeasterly territory was mountainous timber country where lumbermen's houses were cantilevered above steep and darkly forested slopes. The eastern coastal section featured rolling hills and farmland. Uninhabited islands were located offshore. The southern coastal area was mining territory. Rolling farmlands extended along the westernmost coast. Small villages, like those now in Switzerland, were sprinkled throughout the outlying areas.

The central region was encircled by sheer cliffs fronting tall mountains, thus separating it from the outlying territories. Within the interior were lush tropical forests out of which rose, like huge columns, flat-topped buttes of land 200 to 500 feet high. Some stood in clusters, others alone.

Cities with buildings constructed of wood, stone, and stucco were built atop the plateaux. They were learning centers devoted to instructing future healers, speakers, and teachers, many of whom would return to the lowlands to provide their services. The only access to the top of a butte was by teleportation from its base. Those who were meant to be there were the only ones able to reach the teaching cities.

Periodically, certain children—guided by dreams, by inner knowing, or by wise ones who were drawn to them—would make their way to the teaching centers. After five, ten, or twenty years—whatever time was appropriate to complete their education—students would return to their homelands to share what they had learned.

The roofs of the high cities were covered with crystals. Rising tall above the misty forests, they shone brilliantly in the sun. Crystal Cities they were called.

The many civilizations of Lemuria evolved culturally and spiritually until there came a time when their destiny on the physical plane had been fulfilled. Each being had a choice of transcending to the higher realms of existence or reincarnating on planet Earth. Many, out of love for humanity, opted to return to begin anew in lifetime after lifetime—each time searching once again for their spiritual path Home.

Those who chose to return held the wisdom and light of Lemuria and the Goddess as a beacon within—one day to shine their light in a darkened world.

Around 70,000 to 60,000 BC the land of Lemuria evaporated into the mist. Lemurian crystals had been programmed with knowledge and seeded throughout the world, just as the returnees would be. Echoes of Lemuria are found in the cultures of Micronesia, Melanesia, and Polynesia.

Atlantis:
Each of the three civilizations of Atlantis eventually became manifestations of masculine energies out of balance with the feminine, where technology and commerce became valued more than the welfare of people. Though each civilization reached the heights of great technological advancement, because of the moral corruption and indifference to human life that prevailed—compounded by a failure to take responsibility for the world they were creating—each was destroyed by natural disasters. It was not nature's attack, nor God's wrath that brought about

their downfall. It was a reality Atlanteans created to demonstrate how the path they had chosen on their collective spiritual journey, had taken them far off course.

First Civilization:
The continent of Atlantis was in the northern hemisphere, in the Atlantic Ocean. The upper third of the continent was separated from the lower two-thirds by a deep and wide valley through which flowed a major river. Beginning about 50,000 BC, groups of primitive humans who essentially killed, ate, and slept, existed there. They were in the realm of human animals.

As the inhabitants evolved into human *beings*—by realizing that there was something more than mere survival—eventually a civilization arose in the southeastern coastal region of the continent. It was an area separated and protected from the rest of the continent by a range of mountains. Over time the City of Atlantis was created along hundreds of miles of its coastline. Other cities arose in areas that were also protected from the more primitive northern region.

As the first Atlantean civilization evolved over several millennia it became more and more technologically oriented, eventually valuing technology and commerce over people's rights.

The destruction of the first civilization of Atlantis occurred around 42,000 BC. It was caused by a series of tremendous earthquakes which produced a chain reaction of fires. Nuclear energy facilities, stadiums, and other significant structures had been built over fault lines and were destroyed. Most inhabitants did not survive.

Second Civilization:
The continent of Atlantis was split into two large land masses by tectonic action during the first destruction. The upper third of the continent split off and remained a primitive island. On the lower portion, once again from rudimentary origins, there evolved a civilization more advanced than any the world had known.

The downfall of this second Atlantean civilization was brought about by political corruption and by seeking and holding on to power for its own sake. The despotic and corrupt government was held together by

martial law—and martial law was used to maintain the level of medioc-
rity that prevailed. Graft paid to allow development of lands lying over
earthquake fault lines helped to set up the conditions for destruction.

The combination of governmental ineptitude, corruption, and martial
law was manifested outwardly as natural disasters—volcanic eruptions,
earthquakes, fires, and tidal waves—that caused the destruction of the
second civilization of Atlantis around 28,200 BC.

Few survived, but those who did escaped in boats and rafts that were
carried along by ocean currents to other lands, where they formed small
pockets of civilization.

Third Civilization:
The second destruction of Atlantis reduced the uninhabited northern
landmass to many small islands, and the lower portion to a grouping of
larger islands. The small islands in the north remained primitive and
mostly uninhabited because of their isolation. The third civilization
evolved once more in the lower areas, and a new City of Atlantis was
established on several big islands.

The third civilization also became highly advanced. Automobiles
were used on the larger islands, but they were impractical on the smaller
ones, and there were powerboats for ocean travel. Cities had skyscrapers
of glass and chrome. Other structures were designed much like Greek
architecture. People used colorful hot-air balloons for extended travel.
Some who flew long distances were aware of the barbarians and prim-
itives living in far off lands.

With the advancements, however, came a loss of respect for human
dignity and for human value, because the emphasis once more was on
technology and commerce at the expense of human rights and human
life. Generally speaking, spirituality was under-developed throughout
their society—stunted by old beliefs. There was a lack of character and
vision. No sense of personal fulfillment. People lost hope and forgot how
to dream. How to imagine.

Poverty, homelessness, and drug addiction were widespread. Those
afflicted were the "forgotten ones." Such people were warehoused. Old
people were exiled to one island. Prostitutes were sent to a separate,
guarded island. Derelicts and addicts were shipped to another and kept

out of sight. Water supplies on any island could be polluted to extermi-
nate the residents and reclaim the land.

There were some who tried in vain to bring about reform. They
included an underground of metaphysicians who opposed the horror,
the damage and destruction that was done to the forgotten ones. They
set up half-way houses to help the homeless and the addicts—many of
them very young. Many spoke out against the government, which was
considered a treasonous act, not understanding that they had the personal power to change their own reality.

The final destruction of Atlantis—caused by earthquakes, tidal waves,
the breaking of natural gas lines, and the resulting pollution—took
place around 10,800 BC. Those events obliterated what was left of the
Atlantean land mass. This time, however, many more escaped. Certain
ones had anticipated the coming destruction and had prepared for it.
Some of them left before the disasters began. Others left at the first signs.

The survivors were like the seeds of their civilization, spreading out
in different directions in hot-air balloons, and on boats and rafts that
followed the ocean currents. Groups of refugees landed on the shores of
Western Europe, Africa, and the Middle East. Some sailed southwest on
currents that carried them to the Yucatan peninsula, barren and inhos-
pitable. From there they migrated to the Americas. The great Mayan,
Incan, and Aztec civilizations arose from Atlantean origins.

Some refugees huddled together in small, isolated communities and
eventually became extinct. Others integrated with the indigenous population and greatly impacted the advancement of their cultures. The
Druids of Great Britain and France emanated from Atlantean influence,
as did the Vikings in Scandinavian lands.

A few of the more advanced Atlantean survivors had the ability to
work with laser beams, which were used extensively in Atlantis. Those
elite groups were the basis of later myths about the mighty Greek and
Norse Gods.

Other Atlantean survivors found their way to Sumar (also known as
Sumer), now called Iraq. Sumerian culture became very advanced and
its influence contributed to discoveries made in Egypt.

Egyptian and Sumerian calendars were based upon the rotation of
the star system Sirius because Atlanteans knew of its significance in our

universe, and therefore its great importance to humanity. July 23rd of each year begins a period of fifty-five days when Sirius is closest to the Earth and its vortex of energy opens wide. It is the etheric portal into our holographic universe. Calendars of Sumar, Egypt, and other ancient cultures began on that date.

Certain Atlanteans first landed in Egypt, but because they loved to travel, they moved on. They came to be known as Gypsies. Other refugees migrated to Egypt from other areas of the Middle East. Egyptian pyramids were built with Atlantean technology using sound waves to pulverize gigantic stone blocks into pebbles, later to be re-assembled in place by again using sound waves.

The pyramids—originally designed to represent the tapering points of Atlantis' huge generator crystals—were constructed so that when the star Sirius is closest to the Earth, its light would shine through pyramid windows designed for that purpose. Pyramids of similar design are found today in the far-flung parts of the world where Atlanteans migrated.

Atlantean refugees also brought with them crystals they had programmed with knowledge—crystals hold energy and emit energy when tapped or rubbed—and buried or scattered them in the areas they visited. They also brought their spiritual and religious beliefs which included the worship of Goddess-God.

The migration of Atlantean survivors produced a dispersion of advanced knowledge throughout the world. Today, standing stones, pyramids, temples, and crystals found around the world are evidence of the influence of Atlantis.

Also by Patty Paul
A NEW SPIRITUALITY: BEYOND RELIGION

❖ ❖ ❖ ❖

What readers have said about *A New Spirituality: Beyond Religion*:

"A veritable toolbox offering many ways to change and empower your life. You'll feel enlivened, challenged and inspired to work with your physical reality as a mirror yielding keys to what internal/external changes are necessary for your evolution."
—K. Pokletar, *Whole Life Times*

"I go back and read parts of the book when I want to feel better."
—S. Wade, writer, Venice, CA

"Thank you again for your book. It's the clearest explanation I could give anyone who doesn't know these higher truths. I gave my copy to an old friend, now I'm off to buy another for myself!" —Beverly Doran, Glendale, CA

"I feel like I just read Cliff's Notes to the universe!" —Ms. A.R., Ventura, CA

"As I read your book, I felt re-inspired regarding my spiritual path. I actually felt a part of me was being nurtured and I felt it resonating with my soul while I was reading."
—Frances Perkins, Los Angeles, CA

"A wonderful book. It's been a steady seller."
—Rod Carney, Crystal Blue Books, Atlanta, GA

"Everyone needs one of these books!"
—Margaret Johnson, Owner, Wings Books & Gifts, Denver, CO

"A particularly valuable chapter on the balance of masculine and feminine energy within each of us can help clear the fog around the effects of chauvinism and feminism." —*The Positive Times*

"Superior Writing! Great!" —Jersey Society of Parapsychology

"I was so excited to finally find this information in a book. I bought your book and read it all that night, then called my brother and told him he *had* to read it! I sent him a copy the next day." —Carol A., Oceanside, CA

"It defines the difference between structured religion and spirituality and offers evidence that a trend toward the latter is now underway." —*New Age Omega Directory*

"Patty Paul has done a wonderful job showing us a universe that is both alive and benevolent. A book I recommend to those seeking the awareness of the divine within."
—Cheri Woods, C.Ht.

"The premise of the book is the concept that each person creates their own reality, therefore they have the power to change it and (the author) tells us how." —*Arizona Networking*

"Patty Paul's book is filled with the essential vitamins and minerals that lead to personal and spiritual growth. The practical advice she gives allows readers to immediately and directly apply her wisdom to their daily lives." —Cathy Collins, *Dream On! Magazine*

"A wonderful book…recommended to anyone ready to change their life for the better." —Marilyn Winfield, MA, Therapist, Pacific Palisades, CA

"I enjoyed it so much, I encourage people to get the book and read it." —Beverly Dennis, Clinical Therapist, Beverly Hills, CA

"I have become enthralled with your book. I read your book with a pencil and a notebook at hand so that I can deepen every facet that I want to register into my brain. It has been of enormous help. Thank you so much." —Pierre de Serres, Toronto, Ontario, Canada

"This book is *so* needed!" —Judy Regan, Owner, New Voyage Bookstore, Rochester, NY

"Down to earth, logically written and as clear as you hoped it would be, *A New Spirituality* will fill an important slot in your resource library." —J. Wescott, *The Positive Times*

"I welcome this book." —Owner, Aurora Borealis Bookstore, Anaheim, CA

"What I was most impressed by was that it was not preachy, more of a guiding light or beacon for those interested. It was easy to read and understand." —Frances Perkins, Los Angeles, CA

"I love this book! I'm buying five more copies for friends." —J. Preston, Huntington Beach, CA

"Written with intelligence, clarity, directness, and love. (It) provides a valuable guide to changing our lives." —V. White, President, White Light Publishing

"This book is brimming with extensively researched and interesting nuggets. (It) is easy to take in and put to use in your life!" —Karina Pokletar, *Whole Life Times*

"This reviewer found *A New Spirituality: Beyond Religion* to be empowering, inspirational, challenging, and healing." —Richard Fuller, *Metaphysical Reviews*

"I enjoyed your great book so much I'm sharing it with a special friend. I bought three more copies for other friends." —Eunice Fleming, Brawley, CA

"I was inspired by a book called "A New Spirituality: Beyond Religion" I borrowed from a fellow inmate. How can I get my own copy?" —Inmate, State Prison, Corcoran, CA

"Brilliant!" —Ms. D.B., Studio City, CA

A New Spirituality: Beyond Religion (ISBN 978-09642726-7-5) is available at Amazon.com.

CPSIA information can be obtained
at www.ICGtesting.com
Printed in the USA
BVHW040803090621
609012BV00007B/1587